YOUR INFINITE POWER

The Hidden Path to Manifesting
Real Freedom & Abundance

YOUR INFINITE POWER

The Hidden Path to Manifesting Real Freedom & Abundance

JANIA AEBI

YOUR INFINITE POWER

The Hidden Path to Manifesting Real Freedom & Abundance

Copyright © 2017, Jania Aebi

The views expressed by the author in reference to specific people in their book represent entirely their own individual opinions and are not in any way reflective of the views of Transformation Catalyst Books, LLC. We assume no responsibility for errors, omissions, or contradictory interpretation of the subject matter herein.

Transformation Catalyst Books, LLC does not warrant the performance, effectiveness, or applicability of any websites listed in or linked to this publication. The purchaser or reader of this publication assumes responsibility of the use of these materials and information. Transformation Catalyst Books, LLC shall in no event be held liable to any party for any direct, indirect, punitive, special, incidental, or any other consequential damages arising directly or indirectly from any use of this material. Techniques and processes given in this book are not to be used in place of medical or other professional advice.

No part of this book may be reproduced or transmitted in any form, or by any means, electronic or mechanical, including photography, recording, or in any information storage or retrieval system without written permission from the author or publisher, except in the case of brief quotations embodied in articles and reviews.

Published by:
Transformation Books
211 Pauline Drive #513
York, PA 17402
www.TransformationBooks.com

ISBN: 978-1-945252-29-7
Library of Congress Control Number: 2017949020

Cover design: Ranilo Cabo
Layout and typesetting: Ranilo Cabo
Editor: Michelle Cohen
Proofreader: Michelle Cohen and Gwen Hoffnagle
Book Midwife: Carrie Jareed
Author Photo: Tania Blanco

Printed in the United States of America

TABLE OF CONTENTS

Foreword 1

Chapter 1:
The One Great Power: Discovering and Accessing It....................5

Chapter 2:
The Power Within: Reclaiming Your Responsibility 41

Chapter 3:
The Power of Self-Awareness:
Changes Must Be Done Now-Here..79

Chapter 4:
The Power of Problems: Using Challenges
to Make You Stronger 109

Chapter 5:
The Power of Manifestation: Getting What You Really Want ...137

Chapter 6:
The Power of Surrender: Releasing All Resistance 169

Chapter 7:
The Power of a Great Life: Activating Your Potential 197

About the Author..221
Notes 223
Resources...225

FOREWORD

It was online that I first met Jania, an energy healer. She was different from most of the people in my programs because she did not want to start or develop a business, write a book, or create a program. She was not interested in any of that. All she wanted was to achieve a deeper conscious connection with God. Of course, this is the greatest goal one can have, and one that is nearest and dearest to my own heart and soul. I knew, however, that she was in for a much bigger vision than merely sitting on a mountaintop somewhere in quiet contemplation. I knew she had some work to do in the world! Despite her insistence that she didn't 'have it in her,' I continued to remind her that there was so much more trying to emerge. And as her connection to the divine deepened, her potential did indeed unfold–including the writing of this book, *Your Infinite Power*.

In her characteristic humility, even after completing this book, a program, and launching her work in the world, she still didn't appreciate what she had accomplished. Yet Jania's capacity to keep moving forward with courage, character, and mastery is a true sight to behold, a testament to the power of the divine connection she writes about. Jania has been a continual inspiration to me and the many people she touches.

Imagine cutting a fully bloomed flower from its branch, its source. You can place it in a crystal vase of water to enjoy its short-lived color and fragrance, but the flower will not generate more blooms because the stem has been severed from its branch, the expression of the plant's life force and power. When in consciousness we cut ourselves off from our Source—God, divinity—we become disconnected from its energy and experience separation, which is the core reason for most of our problems and issues. The understanding of this, and the journey to reconnect with this source, is what Jania teaches so masterfully in *Your Infinite Power*.

The wish and the impulse to assist and help others in their struggles with life's challenges did not come early, or easily to Jania, but were something that grew out of her own encounters with situations she was faced with on the continents of Europe and Africa. She has known conditions of wars and ethnic disturbances from her earliest childhood. While Jania suffered the personal loss of most of her family, her husband, and then her only son, she has found the courage to rebuild her life on a basis that is more solid than the moving sands of personal human considerations.

Jania's journey is proof that a complete turnaround in life need not take decades or even a long time. After being retired for ten years, she started on a new path that had nothing to do with her previous life. Jania had to learn new skills, develop a new mindset, and launch in a totally new direction. It is proof that it's never too late to start again, whatever the circumstances, especially when you have the connection to Source that she writes about in her book.

As consciousness evolves in an ever-widening capacity, Jania's healing abilities also evolved to transmitting Source energy to larger audiences. At a certain point, Jania realized that she needed a tool to reach even more people–and her book was born. *Your Infinite Power* encourages every reader to take the healing of their life into their own hands by understanding that they are not merely a human being, but rather a soul that has gifted them with all that it is. Jania guides us to first peel away the wrapping of our own unconscious and limiting beliefs to find the true beauty of who we really are.

Jania keeps readers rooted in spirit and teaches how to manifest thoughts through actions and how to be conscious creators. She suggests how to access the power of spirit in every life situation. *Your Infinite Power* is filled with brilliant anecdotes and eloquent explanations of consciousness and quantum physics that guide readers into discovering how to consciously reconnect to Source

FOREWORD

and live in its pure unity. Jania draws upon her rich life experiences and vast knowledge of divinity and non-duality to help readers change their perceptions and frequency. She offers advice, exercises, and meditations to help readers shift from being victims of events and circumstances to reclaiming their mental, emotional, and spiritual power.

The Universe always works for us, not against us. Based on this principle, readers will recognize the gift or learn the lesson in order to align with the perspective of Source. If we can develop our self-awareness, we can see the deeper meaning of challenges. Part of this self-awareness is the understanding that some beliefs and conditions of early childhood are filters that keep us powerless. Jania walks with us through our traumatic experiences to find healing and balance by showing readers how to take responsibility for choosing only thoughts that serve them.

"Divine qualities become material things when brought into the physical world through action," writes Jania. She believes that our focus, perceptions, and beliefs, which are the only things we can change, determine our experience. When we are at one with Spirit consciousness, we can change our life. *Your Infinite Power* teaches us about the potential of manifestation and getting what we really want in life. In essence, it's your awareness and then your actions that make the attributes of Spirit manifest in your experience. Jania shows us how to see from the perspective of Source rather than from the human perspective, even when things are seemingly not working for us in our lives.

Your Infinite Power brilliantly explains abstract concepts for those unfamiliar with the subject and offers insights that are not usually thought of. This book invites meditation and reflection on where in their own lives people have given away their power and offers ways to reclaim it. Jania's stories create a sense of intimacy and a strong feeling of trust where everyone, whatever their experiences, can rise out of victimhood and build a life that they really want for themselves.

Beyond all of this, what makes this book unique is the emphasis placed on the notion of service to others and how it helps us become more of what our soul is. Even if we all live in our own worlds, we are also visitors in everyone else's worlds, striving to bring more light into any darkness encountered. In these times of global changes and upheavals, we must, more than ever, stay rooted in the only place where we can find stability, support, safety, and security–in our eternal, divine nature.

Derek Rydall, author of *Emergence* and creator of the "Emergence" model

CHAPTER 1

THE ONE GREAT POWER:
DISCOVERING AND ACCESSING IT

Once upon a time, in a far-off magical land, there was an orchard of apple trees that gave its fruit generously, year after year, to Steven and Sharon who looked after the trees, trimmed away the dead branches, nourished the soil, watered, and weeded it. Now it was spring, and the trees were in full bloom. Everywhere you looked, each branch was covered with delicate white flowers touched with pink at the edges. The leaves were barely visible, just a tinge of green here and there.

It was a beautiful day, the sun inviting many little creatures and bees to come out of hiding and go about their daily business. And that, mostly, was all about feeding themselves, their families, or communities, drinking from dewdrops, collecting pollen to fill honeycombs with honey, constructing beautiful intricate spider webs that glistened in the morning sun.

Sunshine and warmth had also brought out many people, coming for a breath of fresh air and to look at the profusion of spring colors bursting everywhere. They sauntered along the paths skirting the orchard, which were smooth and easy to walk on. Sharon and Steven had also come out, as they did most mornings, but for them it was not enough to just look at the trees from a distance. They wanted a closer look to take in the fragrance of the blooms; to watch as the bees landed on open flowers, getting their little feet coated in pollen; to search for any signs of mold on the new foliage.

They went deeper and deeper into the orchard, admiring every tree, each branch different from the one next to it, but just as beautiful.

"Let's take one of those branches back with us. I want to remember how this looked even when I'm home!" exclaimed Sharon.

"Let's do that," replied Steven, "but first, we'll look around to find a special one, the one we really like best."

The trees heard this and started getting anxious; they liked getting rid of the dead wood, but were not so sure about a live limb being cut off. Being magical, the branches could also talk, so started whispering to each other:

"What's going to happen to the one that's cut off?"

"We will no longer be together."

"I hope it's not me they take . . . ."

"Can we survive if we are no longer connected to the tree?"

"The one they take will surely be the most beautiful . . . ."

But one of the branches was thinking differently, thinking just of itself, how limited it was here, and what experiences it could have when on its own out in the world, and said, "I want to be the one they take home! I've had enough of being stuck here. I can make it on my own! Look how strong and beautiful I am: I don't need the tree any longer; I don't need help from anyone. I want to see the world! When I was small, the tree supported me, but now I've grown so much, I have all I need. I'm just as powerful as the tree, and I will be fine!"

"I still think we need the tree . . . what will it be like to be cut off . . . I would rather stay with my parent . . . !" On and on the branches went, until one deeper voice came through from an older, thicker, and wiser branch than all the others, carrying a deeper message.

"Don't you know that our life is the life of the tree? That we're all beautiful in our own way? No one is more beautiful than another: we're just different; we take our life from this huge trunk to which we're all connected. If a branch is separated, if it's taken away, what will happen to it? How will it live?"

"I have enough strength to be on my own," insisted the rebel branch, "and I also have beauty and confidence and such an abundance of buds as none of you have; so I will make sure I'm the one they will take!" And helped by the breeze, it leaned towards the couple, hoping to be chosen.

And it was.

Steven cut the branch he had just noticed. With a small bow, he handed it to Sharon, saying, "The most beautiful branch for the most beautiful lady! It has so many buds. We'll enjoy it for many days."

The branch turned to its brothers and sisters and said, "You see, I'll be fine! I will see the world outside, and I will still be looked after and admired, not like here, where there's no one to see me. I can make it on my own, without anyone's help. I don't need the tree any more, it's given me everything it has, and I will live my own life, be free!"

And so the branch was carried away, put in a vase with lots of fresh water. But somehow, life was different now; it seemed to have less and less strength. It was admired all right, but that didn't last long. Its petals started falling; the leaves wouldn't come out. It was feeling weaker and weaker and at last realized it had no strength and no life of its own. It had not known where the source of its life and strength came from. And so it withered and died, while all the other branches, even if they, too, lost their flowers, remained in place where they bore a rich harvest of fruit that would be repeated over and over, for many years to come.

Just like that self-centered blooming branch, when we have separated ourselves from the real source of power, our capacities diminish, and we will wither and die. But when we stay consciously and mindfully connected to Source, our capacities are almost unlimited. As we progress, you will see that an imagined separation is the core reason for most of our problems and issues.

They stem from our sense of being cut off from God or Divinity; and the most effective, permanent solution is to consciously reconnect to the source of this Real power, our Source.

There Is Only One Power

At some point, we are impelled to examine what, and where, is the source of our life. More fortunate than the branch, we can at any time reconnect to that one source of all power through our awareness and attention to it.

But in order to know how powerful you really are, you must at least be open to the possibility that there is a Source of your being that is invisible, omnipotent, omniscient, and omnipresent, called Spirit or God or Life or Source–whatever name you want to give it–and that you are always connected to it. That in fact you are it, because when life leaves the body in what we call death, our consciousness is still functioning and aware, even if it no longer experiences sensations through the body.

When you really understand you are Spirit, or Consciousness beyond your body, it follows that the body is in your consciousness, not the other way round. So everything in your awareness must of necessity be in your Consciousness. As a physical body, basically, you're only aware of what you can see, hear, taste, smell, or touch. And this includes mind and the things we have learned without actually seeing them. But if you allow for the possibility that Spirit is everything there is, and therefore you as Consciousness are an expression of that Spirit in the material realm, then you know Consciousness encompasses the whole Universe, whether as a physical being you know about it, or not.

That Consciousness which you are has endowed you at birth with free will and with a spiritual awareness that no other expression of the divine in this world has. Everything is an expression of Divinity; but humans are the only ones in this world who have a spiritual awareness and free will to choose. Whatever name we give it, we are all aware of something bigger, more powerful, and wiser than us, that makes the Universe function perfectly. Your mind and body are just expressions in more and more density of the wholeness of that Spirit.

Your Source is spiritual, so it expresses itself in a spiritual Reality, that of your soul, made in the image and likeness of God, having all knowledge, all power, present everywhere, infinite, eternal, and invisible. It's a perfect expression of the universal energy where there is no time, no space, no distance as we know it, and so there is no experience of anything.

Time, space, and duality are constructs or perceptions that allow the Pure Spirit to have an experience of its All-ness, one experience after another. Everything that is visible and changing and moving has been projected by the soul so as to have an experience; and you, as a human being living your life are an avenue, or an instrument through which Spirit can have that experience.

Of course Spirit has experiences through every blade of grass, flower, animal, and visible thing, but we are the only species with self-awareness. So the individual called John or Sue is just a feedback mechanism for events to be experienced by Consciousness, what we call our soul. In everyday life, we identify primarily–and very often solely–with the material self. And since pure spirit lives in unity with Source, "your" soul and "their" soul are one, within that Source of all power.

All great religions have told us that. In the Bible it says, "Hear, O Israel: The Lord our God, the Lord is one." (Deuteronomy 6:4) The Koran, also based on monotheism, says, "Worship Allah alone and keep away from all false deities."[1] The theme of the oneness of Source is seen throughout all the main scriptures of the world, and oneness cannot be divided into parts. We see ourselves as separate from each other and from Source; but if we saw from the perspective of Spirit, we would perceive only the wholeness and perfection of everything, just expressing as different forms in the time/space construct of our world.

We can begin to see from the perspective of Source rather than from the human perspective, even when things are not working. Imagine an ant climbing a huge hill–from your perspective, a molehill–going over dry twigs, fallen leaves, and all manner of obstacles hoping to find some food that is nowhere in sight. It cannot see beyond its limited vision, stopped by the next leaf or twig. But you, from your higher vantage point, can see the breadcrumbs on the other side of that molehill. To the ant, its lunch is in the future and in the distance, maybe not even a reality depending on the path it takes. But for you, the ant, the crumbs, and yourself are all in your present reality. We are like the ant, not aware of the expanded perspective.

Science Catches Up with Spiritual Teachings

What religion has always taught, quantum physics is now proving: that there is a unified field of energy and information that underlies all manifestation, a field of pure potential that is invisible and interpenetrates and connects all visible things. There is no such thing as empty space. Everything emerges from that field and sinks back into it. Under certain conditions, it becomes denser and takes on form, becomes visible. When those conditions no longer apply, the form disintegrates back into formless potentiality. Science now is proving what ancient religious texts have always told us.

Science defines the quantum field *as one, infinite, eternal, and invisible*; and strangely enough, that is precisely the definition of God, as given by the mystics and great religions of the world. So we must conclude that they are one and the same thing, whatever name we give it. The first expression of that Spirit, or field of energy, is spiritual, therefore invisible, infinite, eternal, and perfect, the spiritual realm, or our soul. It's indivisible from that underlying field of energy, just a slightly denser expression. Therefore, the soul has all the power and wisdom of Spirit, and there is no power outside of it to change or destroy it.

The theory of entanglement says that everything is always connected to everything else. When one entangled particle receives a stimulus, the other, even thousands of miles away, will react in that same moment. So ultimately, if everything is one, power is also one.

Let me illustrate this for you. You are a community of fifty trillion cells, or more! Starting from one cell separating itself at conception, you become the whole of you. The cells have combined in specific ways to form fingers, an arm, a foot, a heart, and every part of your body, from the smallest to the largest.

Now imagine that every part of your body has self-consciousness, and the fingers think it is their power that holds your cup of coffee upright. The legs think their power is to walk. The mouth thinks it decides when to open and when to close. From their level of consciousness, it certainly looks this way, and they don't know that the only power they have to function at all is from your mind and intention.

Take this idea one level up: your consciousness (hopefully!) can tell you that the only power you have to function at all comes from the Mind of Spirit that incarnated in you. Because when Spirit leaves, what is called "death," you can no longer do anything that up to now you thought *you* were doing!

Take this one level up again: you, as a whole being, constitute one cell in the larger community called humanity. Just as your cells cooperate with each other for your well-being, you must cooperate with other people for the well-being of humanity. There are infinitely more layers like that to explore until you get to the top–ultimate Unity with the Love, Wisdom, and Power of Source. That One power is then stepped down through all the layers; so there is no power outside of Source, even if it looks like that to a limited consciousness.

All the laws governing the formed Universe are also already in existence; however, they simply are not visible to our physical senses. They exist as a potential. In other words, the laws of the harmonic scale, electricity, and aerodynamics have always been here, no one invented them, but the consciousness of the Neanderthal man was not developed enough to discover and apply them.

The nature of that unified field of energy can be termed "perfection," in the sense that there is nothing other than it and nothing less than it. It is perfect not in the moralistic sense of goodness, but in the sense of completeness. The unified field is all joy, beauty, harmony, health, abundance, love, and every quality you can think of, with no possibility of a negation. And if you reflect deeply enough on any quality, you will find it reduces to just one idea: love. Divine Love is one and cannot be divided; it never varies and never changes. What we humans call love is a feeling, an emotion, not the very substance of the Universe that never changes. Our love changes day by day, depending on conditions.

"You've forgotten our wedding anniversary, so I love you less today than yesterday . . . "

"You haven't given me what I wanted, I don't love you any more . . . "

"I love you, because . . . "

This is how we feel and act, even if we don't say it, and that kind of love is not part of Reality with a capital "R." The only Reality is eternal, therefore always there; infinite, therefore has no beginning and no end; unconditional, therefore not dependent on conditions; and spiritual, therefore invisible.

THE ONE GREAT POWER: DISCOVERING AND ACCESSING IT

There Is Reality and reality

Hopefully, all this has allowed you to realize that what seems to exist and then changes has no Real existence. The only Reality is the underlying energy from which everything material arises, and into which all materiality dissolves. If you look at anything in the world, you can see continual change and transformation. Look at a flower: it's here one day, has fallen off the next, and then becomes part of the earth, the nutrient for the roots in its vicinity. Look at a star: it's here for millions of years, but in the end it either implodes or explodes, and its life as a star is over. The existence of everything visible will no longer exist as it is now in a day, a year, a hundred or a million years from now. It will have become something else, even down to just a potential.

> What seems to exist and then changes has no Real existence.

Look closer at yourself: you started off in a baby body, which over some years became you at the age of ten. You were quite sure you were really you, right? And then look at yourself at the age of twenty. You were equally sure that was you. Look at yourself now: not one single cell in your body is the same cell that was there when you were ten or twenty, yet you still feel that you are basically the same You, the one Spirit you always were. You are like the wave on the ocean, appearing different, but always part of the one ocean.

Real power comes from the source of your being. Remember that branch covered in flowers? It didn't realize all its strength and beauty came from the life force starting at the roots and going up the trunk–it just looked at itself, wanting to be admired for itself, thinking the power was within itself. For the branches left on the tree, the flowers turned into fruit and seed and then the tree rested for a while before the life force gathered again for the branches to bloom year after year, giving new fruit every time. The severed branch withered and died.

The same principle applies to human beings. Living our lives on the material level alone is being that severed branch. If we recognize the spiritual part of us, underlying the physical part, then we connect to the Spirit that is love, joy, harmony, and perfection, and experience more and more of its qualities. The only permanence for nature is in its roots; the only permanence for humanity is in its spiritual roots, through conscious awareness of that connection.

It is said that one day, the disciples of the mystic Yogananda came to ask him, "Master, what is real?" And he answered, "That is Real which never changes."[2] Think that through–and see if there is anything Real to your everyday life. Understand that the spiritual Reality cannot be proved by our finite five senses; it can only be felt.

As far back as our history goes, we notice humanity has had this perception of a division of the one presence and one power, as in the Greek or Roman pantheon of gods. Each of them represented some core quality of the one Spirit. Hercules represented strength; Venus represented beauty. We also gave them human, less-than-good qualities, because we live in a time/space construct called duality, where we only know good because there is bad; we only know light because there is dark; we only know up because there is down.

Imagine living in the center of the sun, surrounded by shadowless light all the time. You have always lived there: your parents and grandparents and all your ancestors have never known anything but living in light. If someone came and said you lived in light, you would just respond, "What is light?" Without an opposite, there is no way of knowing what light is.

THE ONE GREAT POWER: DISCOVERING AND ACCESSING IT

Attributes of Spirit

From all of the above, emerge three core ideas about Spirit: that it is omnipotent, omniscient, and omnipresent, which means –

- it has all power, so there is no power outside of it to change or destroy it;
- it has all knowledge, so there is no knowledge beyond it, and science has now proved this through the theory of entanglement; and
- it is everywhere present, so there can be nothing in which it is not, and nothing that is outside of it.

Except for a very few thinkers and philosophers, such as Socrates and Plato, the average consciousness of the Greek or Roman times could not conceive of a unified field of energy that was perfect love. The present consciousness has evolved and, for the most part, accepts monotheism, that God is one, even if some religions still attribute Him human qualities such as He is vengeful, He is to be feared, He punishes us, and that He requires our love. I believe He requires no such thing, seeing us as one with Him. Do you require your hand to love you? Or do you just consider it a part of you?

Every material manifestation arises from the spiritual realm, so behind every "thing" lies the invisible spiritual matrix. Under certain conditions energy becomes solidified; so our mind and thoughts are energy in fluid form, while matter, things, are energy in a solid, dense form. I once heard an easy way to remember that all is one: "Mind is matter in liquidity, and matter is mind in solidity."

So for example, say you wanted to build a house. It all starts with desire and imagination: every structure was once imagined, and is the answer to a need. Your desire becomes a focused thought on what it will look like, how big it's going to be, how to achieve it, how much it would cost, how to get the money, and where to build it. Once those ideas are clear, you make a blueprint of the house. Now you're out of the realm of pure thought into thought + action: you need to calculate, draw, imagine the materials that will be best, and use some actual physical paper to move forward. The next stage is getting the actual physical stuff you will need, then physically putting it together so it becomes the house you once imagined.

What was in your imagination becomes a physical reality under certain conditions, which are: continuing to hold your desire with determination; being open and receptive to new ideas that might come; and taking inspired action–that feels good and in alignment with Spirit, not action from a place of frustration or desperation that nothing is appearing as yet. You trust that the Spirit, from which your desire came, manifests equally as your thought and as the material things needed. Leave the timing of the material manifestation to Spirit, while you watch for the openings that feel right for moving forward into action.

Energy and Its Material Manifestation Are Indivisible

Action is always required when dealing with dense forms of manifestation, but which are not separate from the spiritual or energetic forms. They are one, just appearing as energy you can see, or energy you cannot see with your physical eyes. When we read in the Bible, "God saw all that he had made and behold, it was very good," (Genesis 1–31) it's referring to the spiritual invisible creation, which is complete and perfect unity: one life, one mind, one substance, one presence, one power. When this spiritual unity is further solidified, it appears as different qualities or different things, depending on the frequency of the vibration.

There is a simple example of this solidification of energy under certain conditions in our physical world. Take water, which at a low temperature will solidify into ice. Its appearance, density, even its form will change, depending on the container. But the inherent qualities of water are still present. If you raise the temperature around that ice, it reverts back into water. If you raise the temperature even higher, at a certain point the water will become steam and disappear from your view. Nothing has changed except the conditions surrounding the water, which made it solidify into certain forms, or made it disappear.

Just as there is an underlying oneness when we look deeper into things we call steam, water, and ice, we will find an underlying Oneness—some quality of Spirit—when we look deeper into any of the material forms surrounding us.

> There is only one infinite presence and power of Spirit that is everywhere. Therefore it must be where you are.

Look at the chair you're sitting on right now: it represents support, comfort, stability, harmony in the lines of its design, perhaps also beauty, and strength.

Look at a horse: it represents service, strength, symmetry, balance, beauty, and I'm sure you can think of many other qualities as well.

Look at a tree: it is abundant in its foliage, strong and resilient, harmonious and beautiful, colorful, serving many other forms of life by providing food and shelter, safety and support.

If you're willing to look, you will find divine qualities in every expression of the energy of life.

That Power Is Where You Are

I hope that you can now feel, and to some degree understand, that there is only one infinite presence and power of Spirit that is everywhere. The corollary to that is, therefore it must be where you are. You are it; you are that Spirit, not your body. To fully realize this, let's do this short mental exercise.

EXERCISE

Put your full attention on your right big toe. Are you in your toe? No, obviously not. Are you your toe? The answer is still no. Now shift your attention to your left knee. Are you in your knee? Or, are you your knee? You know you are not your knee, either. And how about your shoulder: are you that shoulder, or is it, in fact, that you have a shoulder? Take your head: are you your head, or in your head? Or do you have a head? You can keep shifting your attention to any part of your body, and you will always find you are not that part. You get my point!

So if you are not any part of your body, you cannot be your body, either. So what and where are you in reality? You have found you never are the toe, knee, or shoulder–you *have* toes, knees, and shoulders. Even our language gives us a clue to that. You say: *my* toe hurts, *my* knee is swollen, and *my* shoulder is broken. It's *your* body. So where is this You, since you've just realized it's not your body?

You is your soul, your Consciousness, an invisible energy that is animating the body; it is breathing you, making all your organs function without your even being aware of it, manipulating objects through your mind and muscles. In fact, your body is within your Consciousness, just as is everything you see, know, and are aware of. You are your Consciousness made in the image and likeness of God. Whatever forms you see–including yourself, your body, and mind–can never be separate from Spirit. In your Consciousness lies all your power.

Given all this, everything that we can see, feel, know, or do is just the expression into materiality of that Source.

Materiality can be more or less dense: just as water can be denser or less dense, appearing as ice or steam. So whatever forms you perceive, whether they are material or mental, can never be separate from the underlying Spirit. And that includes you. Potentially, you always have all its knowledge and wisdom, its health, wealth, harmony, joy, and power at your disposal. You have been given a higher awareness than the rest of creation, but you must know where to access it in order to create the experiences you want. Otherwise you will live an unconscious life, buffeted by external conditions.

Lack Is a Function of Feeling Separate from Source

You experience lack in its many forms when you believe you are separate from God, and therefore separate from the wholeness He is. You think you must get what you want from outside of you. You believe that people or circumstances have power over you, when in reality you actually give away your power to others. The belief you are not Spirit and do not have all its qualities is the one great power leak that is the source of all your problems and suffering. If that leak is stopped, it's your gateway to a rich, happy, and fulfilled life.

When you are fully aware of being just an expression of that unified field of energy, you can no longer envisage being in conflict with any other part of that field. You are one with every part of it. Conversely, so long as you do feel a conflict with any other expression of that field, whether it's a person, situation, or thing–and that includes internal conflict with yourself–you cannot experience the oneness in which lie all the things you most want. It's impossible. When you reduce conflict, your experience automatically reflects more of the Spirit that you are.

Once you become aware of Spirit being the real You, if only for a fleeting moment, you cannot un-know it. You will feel it more, or feel it less, depending on the external conditions facing you, but you cannot un-know it. The knowledge that there is only one life, one mind, one power, will always be at the root of your consciousness. The more you can live from that perspective and the more you can apply it in your everyday life, the more real it will become for you.

As Consciousness, you can be everywhere. We can understand this better now than ever before, with the advent of the Internet on the planet. Two hundred years ago, You as your consciousness could only communicate with another person if you were physically present with them. Otherwise, you travelled by horse-and-buggy, by ship, or train to see them, or you sent a letter. Now, with cell phones, videos, and the Internet, we can transmit our ideas, and, through video, almost *be* with another person instantly, even when they're thousands of miles away. Your consciousness can be where you are now and also be with many other people on the other side of the planet because we have now built physical structures to support greater access to the attributes of omniscience and omnipresence. The attribute of omnipotence is lagging behind, but it only needs our awareness and belief for it to manifest.

And here is another important distinction: what you know, are aware of, and believe, manifests *to you* through the structures you build, either internal or external. They're available to you, not to anyone else. People may be aware, know of, and believe there is such a thing as the Internet, but unless they have the necessary outer structures, for them it remains in the realm of unmanifested possibilities.

Conscious Awareness Enhances the Activity of Source within You

The omnipresence of Spirit focuses in you, and it must flow through you to your world–and through everyone and everything else to their worlds. It has no other means of expressing itself. Similarly, the branch is an expression of the life force of the tree, and has within it the power of the tree. It is said that the Sanskrit word for *man* or *human* meant "the dispenser of divine gifts."[3] We are here to dispense all divine qualities into the material world. Where you are is the presence, the knowledge, and the power of Spirit. In essence, it's your awareness and then your actions that make the attributes of Spirit manifest in your experience. Unless you're aware of something, it's of no use to you.

To illustrate this, I like to use the analogy of John, living in a house inherited from his parents, and even great-grandparents. It's a large house with an old wine cellar that John has turned into storage space. It also has an attic, taking up the whole width and length of the house. Here, his parents had put away things belonging to their parents. When they passed on, John needed space for his own family and belongings, so he also stored things that he just couldn't part with. In fact, the attic and the cellar are full of stuff, and John no longer even knows what's there.

It has been many years: the cost of living has gone up, taxes have gone up, the kids have grown, and there are college fees to pay. It's been harder and harder to keep up with expenses. John has often thought of making a garage sale of everything that's stored, including stuff he didn't need or use. There could even be some valuable antiques, worth a lot of money, stored there. But he pushed the thought aside, procrastinated, felt unmotivated, and kept putting it off till he had more energy. Somehow there was never enough time to really get started. There was too much stuff; he was tired in the evenings and needed his weekends to relax.

At work, there had been rumors that the company would be reducing its staff, and now John had received his letter of notice. This was a blow and totally unexpected. Visions came up of searching for another job, how to survive the gap if he didn't get one immediately, and how to get some extra money. Then the thought of a garage sale came back. Since soon he would no longer be going to the office, John would have time to sort out everything that could possibly be sold.

And that's what he did as soon as he was laid off. Trip after trip, John took down as much as he could carry. Some things went in the trash, some into the garage, which was practically overflowing when he happened to notice an old briefcase that looked as if it had something inside. Maybe there are some family documents there, or maybe the memoirs of some ancestor? He really needed to see what was inside before deciding what to do with it–so he laid it on a nearby table to open it. He could hardly believe his eyes! Packets and packets of $100 bills were neatly stacked in the briefcase. There must have been thousands of dollars–a million or more! He always had plenty of money, but until he knew it, it didn't do him any good.

In the same way, Spirit and its love, joy, harmony, success, health, and wealth exist within you, but are of no use until you become aware and know the key that will open the floodgates of abundance into your life. Your true nature is that powerful and abundant Spirit. You will experience Spirit's gifts in your material life to the degree that you believe it, know it, activate it through your attention, and build the necessary structures. As it says in the Bible: "I and my Father are one" (John 10:30) . . . all I have is yours and all You have is mine." (John 17:10)

All Creation Already Is, But May Not Be Manifested As Yet

Everything has already been created and exists in the spiritual world. Our soul only knows the eternal principles of life that never change, such as the laws of love, unity, the musical scale, mathematics, and gravity, to name but a few. No one ever invented them, they were always here, always active, and if we live in accordance with them, whether consciously or unconsciously, we experience their perfection. They were discovered and consciously applied to fill certain needs, became expressed in words, and had scientific explanations attached to them. But before that happened, people did not step off cliffs because they knew something bad would result if they did; they didn't call it the law of gravity, but lived in harmony with it. People did not believe that 2 + 2 = 3, or they would have been shortchanged all their lives. Certain musical notes placed at a given distance from each other and played together would always produce dissonance, so they did not play those two notes together. Other notes, placed a different distance apart, would produce harmony that was pleasant, so they played those together.

As our consciousness expands, we will be discovering more and more of those laws and, over time, making what now seems impossible, possible.

Since your true nature is infinite, all possibilities are included in it. It cannot be altered in any way, cannot be augmented or diminished by conditions or circumstances. The Bible already refers to that awareness: "He that dwells in the secret place of the Most High shall abide under the shadow of the Almighty . . . A thousand shall fall at thy side, and ten thousand at thy right hand; but it shall not come nigh thee . . . " (Psalm 91). Basically, this means that when you are connected with your Source, there is no other power to diminish, destroy, or harm you in any way. Even when conditions seem destructive, the person with a strong, conscious spiritual connection will not be touched by those conditions, while others may lose everything. When you really *know* the condition facing you–whether you like it or not–is what's best for your evolution, you don't judge it as bad. You accept what it is so that you can become stronger, more inventive, compassionate, wiser, and more aware of the Spirit that is within you. After a while, you reach the point where you become curious every time there is a seemingly adverse situation, because you know it's an opportunity to grow in some way, and it's there for you, not against you.

When your thoughts are aligned with those of Spirit, when your frequency matches, or at least comes close to the frequency of Spirit, then infinite abundance, health, and wealth can freely flow to you and through you into your world simply because the point of expression of that Spirit *for you* is where you are–not at any other point. Even things you don't much like are only there as a reminder that somewhere you are not seeing as Spirit sees, because any appearance is in effect an answer to your prayers or desire for peace, love, harmony, or abundance to manifest. It's just taking a different path to what you might have imagined.

Remember the analogy of finding money in the attic. Times were hard, John needed more money, and what happened was he lost his job. That didn't look like an answer to his prayers! However, it gave him the motivation–and the time–to sort through all the stuff in the attic, and the outcome was beyond his expectations.

Your False Beliefs Stand in the Way of Your Well-Being

So your conscious awareness of who you are, where you stand, and that everything is always conspiring for your good are key elements for your well-being. Those who have not developed this consciousness may not have well-being, but it's their responsibility to achieve that. Helping them materially may work temporarily, but they will always manifest another problem until they change their perspective. The best way to permanently assist anyone is to point them towards spiritual evolution; then it's up to them to make that connection and live in it. If they don't, their sense of separation and the resulting false beliefs will be stopping the spiritual flow of perfection into their world.

It's like when you want to water your garden and only a trickle of water comes through the hose. You open the faucet more and more, but still you get hardly any water. Then you check the hose, see a number of kinks in it, and go about untwisting them one by one. Every time you've straightened out one section, a little more water can flow out; so you keep untwisting and when you get to the last one–maybe even the one before last–you suddenly get the

THE ONE GREAT POWER: DISCOVERING AND ACCESSING IT

whole rush of water coming through. The force of the water was such that when there was just one little kink left, the pressure, all on its own, opened up that last bit.

In the same way, the power and perfection of Spirit is always fully flowing, but your many false and limiting beliefs are like the kinks in the garden hose. As you recognize and start changing them–unkinking the hose–you access more and more of the gifts of Spirit, until the most basic false belief, your sense of separation from the divine, can be swept out of you with a rush of the divine energy. You have full control of only your own garden hose, not anyone else's. You can tell them what's wrong when they don't get to water their garden, but it's up to them to unkink their own water hose.

> Spirit's agenda is for you to grow more like it, express more of its qualities alongside getting the human necessities.

Your sense of separation from Spirit is called the ego. In the first part of this chapter, we have seen the nature of God is Unity. So the ego is not part of Spirit, rather it is your belief in separation, which keeps you focused on material life.

When you live from the standpoint of the ego, just getting more stuff, validation, or support from outside to satisfy your ego's demands, you will never have lasting happiness or joy. Spirit's agenda is for you to grow more like it, express more of its qualities alongside getting the human necessities. Unfortunately, it's only when we have had enough insoluble, painful experiences that we turn to Spirit for solutions. When life is easy and pleasant, the tendency is to sink into materiality and forget spirituality.

Newborn babies have no sense of separation; they still know themselves as Spirit, and they are one with everything, including their mothers. Only at about the age of two do they start differentiating themselves, and that is the reason for what has been termed "the terrible twos," which is their first existential crisis, a realization of being separate. This is the birth of the ego, which over time is developed and strengthened, creating what are called "shadows" through the decisions we make: "I am this" or "I am not that." I will be talking more about these shadows in a later chapter, as they're a very important part of our development.

Spirit will always find a way to make you realize that everything you really desire is a conscious connection with it, a conscious knowing that all good comes from it and cannot come into your material world except *through* you, because you are the instrument through which Spirit expresses itself. It's the qualities of Spirit that become visible things for you. Joy can become a partner for one person, but a speedboat for another. When you are filled with joy, abundance, and well-being, they emerge as the things that make *you* happy–whether it's a partner, money, or a house.

Activating Internal Peace Even in Painful Situations

As long as you live in a consciousness of separation, not realizing that all the power of divinity is exactly where you are, you will experience lack, limitation, disease, and poverty. They will grow more and more pronounced until you start to notice that whenever your attention goes back to Spirit you feel happier, your issues are forgotten at least for a little while, and your experiences become better and better–even if you are still in the same job, the same relationship, and the same neighborhood you so wish you were out of.

You become aware that the source of joy, harmony, and happiness is not in the material world that is clamoring for your attention. Take the time, only a few minutes perhaps, to send your love and appreciation to the divinity that is omnipresent and, therefore, logically where you are. Notice and appreciate the things in your

THE ONE GREAT POWER: DISCOVERING AND ACCESSING IT

life. You have a refrigerator full of food, a car to get around in, even if it's not your dream car. The sun is shining. The rain is watering your plants. You have instant communication with family, friends, and colleagues through email or phone. You have the ability to see and hear, to walk and run. Many do not have that. During all the time spent noticing, appreciating, and thanking, you are connected to Spirit; you are letting the energy of Spirit flow through you just as water flows through a garden hose without any kinks in it.

Even if your life right now seems worse than it has ever been, and you can't find a single redeeming feature in it that makes you happy, there is still something you can do to reach a place of peace and connection, without which nothing can ever change for the better in your life.

All you have to do is turn your attention to a different topic. Think back to some happy event or situation in the past: that birthday celebration when you were six years old; getting that diploma when you finished college; the first time you fell in love and went on that amazing trip together; or looking into the eyes of your newborn child. You could think of what it would be like to win the lottery, all the things you'll be able to do, to have, to experience . . . . Just relive in your mind any happy event, soak in that feeling, and you will notice that the despondency of your present situation has faded away and has been replaced by the joyful emotion of that past event, in the present.

Notice how your mood has changed with those new thoughts; your sadness or upset has disappeared, even if there has been no change in your actual circumstances. You can generate any feeling you want, regardless of circumstances. That's not to say you never deal with an unpleasant situation; you absolutely do, when it's time to be doing that. But at other times, when you find yourself just dwelling in sadness or upset, give yourself permission to change your thoughts to more positive ones. Sometimes that's all that's needed: permission to be happy in spite of circumstances that can't be helped by feeling sad or despondent.

The more you can stay in the consciousness that Source is absolute well-being, and you as part of Source are also in well-being, the more outside circumstances will reflect well-being to you, according to your desires. You will be living your soul's purpose, expressing your unique gifts and talents, and that will leave no room for any negativity.

It's whom you identify with that matters: either with Spirit, which puts you in your spiritual power, or with the body, which leaves you in lack and limitation. Without the life and energy of Spirit, the body on its own is just inert matter, similar to the branch cut off from the tree. When you look at only what the body needs and wants, and neglect spiritual values such as kindness, integrity, consideration, and service, you give away your power–either to people or circumstances–to be happy, fulfilled, and free. You have stepped away from unity with divinity and into duality where your experiences will necessarily show up sometimes as good, sometimes not so good. This does not mean you stop attending to your physical needs; of course you need to eat, and sleep, buy clothes, and see friends. But your main internal focus stays on how can I show more love or be of more help? How can I give a smile to a stranger or a compliment to a friend–or the other way around? Maybe the stranger needs a compliment and the friend, just a smile.

When you smile or make a compliment, it's really hard to remain angry or upset because your mood immediately lightens. You feel happy, considerate, and expansive. These emotions have raised your vibration or frequency just a bit, and you experience compassion for that beggar in the street when the person next to you, frowning, feels the beggar shouldn't be allowed here. The feelings you have determine your frequency.

THE ONE GREAT POWER: DISCOVERING AND ACCESSING IT

Everything Is Frequency and There Are Infinite Frequencies

Every problem resides at a certain frequency; when a problem surfaces, it simply means that your frequency has dropped to a place where problems exist–or rather, to a place where you start judging something as a problem. In other words, you on the one hand, in the space where that problem exists, and Spirit on the other hand, in some other place where no problem exists. In consciousness, you have separated yourself from divinity. When you consciously reidentify with the divinity that's everywhere–where you are and where the problem is–then the only problem is your judgment of it. As you start understanding this by changing your thoughts and perspective, you raise your frequency back to a place where problems cannot exist for you. They still exist for those who live at the frequency of those problems, but you are free.

This is like when ice seems to be a problem where you live–an analogy often used by Derek Rydall. Ice lives at 32°F, and as long as you also live at that temperature, you will never solve the problem of ice. You can chip it away, or melt it with boiling water, to temporarily solve your problem. But very soon, that water will become more ice–a bigger problem. You cannot solve the problem of ice at the frequency, or temperature of 32°F. But as soon as you rise to a higher frequency, it becomes slush, less of a problem. And if you rise again, it just dissolves, disappears, there is no more problem.

In the same way, if you raise the frequency you are at currently, where there might be issues causing you suffering and distress, they will dissolve and disappear from your life, even if they still exist for the person standing next to you. This is because you have placed your attention on what the present opportunity is for you to grow spiritually, on how to think more often of the beauty, joy, and harmony that you see around you, and consequently have forgotten–more and more often and for longer periods–that you have a problem. Every time it comes up again, as it will, pause for a moment, put a "STOP" sign on your racing thoughts, and look at that feeling of inadequacy, not good enough, or that part of you that is in physical distress, and love it as if it were a little child in pain. You cannot make the pain go away, but you can hold the child, love it, and be with it for as long as it needs you. Hold that anxious or suffering part of you to your heart, loving it, thanking it for the message it's sending you, even if you don't fully understand it. Then turn your attention back to the truth of your being, trusting that all physical and material needs will be resolved.

This is the first thing to do; and now that you have raised your frequency closer to that of Spirit, it's time to start looking at what you can do, in the material world, to find a solution for your issue. You have placed yourself in a space where Spirit is, and you now have access to more of its knowledge and its solutions, which you could not see when in the lower vibration of pain, lack, or resentment.

We have been told this over and over in the Scriptures, and the Master Jesus has put it this way: "For the Gentiles eagerly seek all these things . . . But seek ye first the kingdom of God and its righteousness; and all these things shall be added unto you." (Matthew 6:32–33)

And "all these things" means, of course, all the material things we need and desire in this world, whether it's health, money, a relationship, a job, or whatever it may be.

That Power Is Your Source of Everything

In the previous two sections, we have seen that there is only one great spiritual power underlying all things and that we cannot be separate from it however hard we try, because it's everywhere. Therefore it's also the source of everything we desire. Nobody, ever, is our source; they are only a channel–just as we are a channel for someone else's good.

THE ONE GREAT POWER: DISCOVERING AND ACCESSING IT

Your connection with Spirit has been there from your birth, or you wouldn't be alive. It actually is your life; death is simply your Consciousness withdrawing from the material body. The body can then no longer move or think or see or hear–all the faculties and attributes that we think are ours have been infused into the body by Spirit so it can experience the world of form.

Think of it this way: Spirit clothes itself in a body in order to become visible and able to function in the world. Spirit is the life of the body. My cat made me really understand this. I once had a pair of slippers that were huge, they looked like tigers or lions–I think mine were lions. And the front of the slipper was, of course, way beyond my toes. I didn't think of that. Walking to the kitchen one morning, my foot accidentally kicked the cat, and he started attacking the slipper. Of course I picked him up, even though he wasn't really hurt, said all the usual things you say to your cat–and thought everything would be fine. And it was. He was fine with me. I had no problem walking around the house all day, until the evening, when I took out my slippers. The cat rushed at the slipper, spitting and clawing. He still remembered the slipper had kicked him, but never got the understanding the real culprit was my foot, not the slipper.

This illustrates how the body is really a manifestation of the invisible divine Spirit, and the more you're aware of that, the more you focus on that one Presence from which everything manifests. It's the source of everything that you think of as you, including your mind. That Presence is also the trinity of all love, all wisdom, and all power, for there is nothing outside of these three attributes. That trinity represents what we call Heaven, the spirit of God in its fullness, which never changes.

Our material world is an unfolding in space and time of the whole and complete spiritual world beyond it, and it's influenced by our choices. The spiritual, infinite, and invisible world always remains perfect. Its expression as a visible world manifests differently, depending on the choices we make in life.

So where you are now must change, and the only question remaining is whether it changes for the better, reflecting your more spiritual views, or for the worse, reflecting materialistic views. The ultimate outcome–union with the divine–is predetermined; but you choose the road that will take you there: easy and comfortable, or difficult and painful. Can you see that the world you experience is a reflection–with a bit, sometimes even a lot of a time lag–of your thoughts, feelings, and behaviors of the past? As you consciously choose thoughts carrying a higher frequency, thoughts that give rise to better behaviors, you will notice your life improving.

Still, we mostly identify with who we think we are–our bodies–and tend to look after the comfort of our bodies more than being in alignment with our souls. If we really think about this, the way we live doesn't make any sense, because without Soul or Consciousness, the body needs nothing. The body not getting what we think it should have causes all suffering. As we switch our identification to being the Consciousness we really are, the important thing becomes the purpose of that Consciousness. In order to fulfill this purpose, the body needs certain things, and it's really nice to have them; however, our main focus must be on first, fulfilling the desires of our Soul. We have been given a promise: "Seek ye first the kingdom of God, and all these things shall be added onto you." (Matthew 6:33) This means that the material stuff shows up easily and effortlessly when we are consistently centered in Source; and the problems we have, which all lie squarely in the material world, don't seem to be there any more; or if they are, they don't bother us as much as they used to.

THE ONE GREAT POWER: DISCOVERING AND ACCESSING IT

Free Will, When Exercised Counter to Spiritual Laws, Produces Limitation

As your focus shifts from purely material to more spiritual, and things seem to work better, you begin to trust that your Source can indeed take care of things for you. When we read in the Scriptures the words of Jesus, "Truly, I say to you, unless you turn and become like children, you will never enter the Kingdom of Heaven," (Matthew 18:3) it simply means that just as a child knows unconsciously that its parents are the source of safety, security, support, and supply, you must know that your divine parent is your source of everything. As adults we have strayed from that state of childlike trust and made the physical self the doer; we must now move back into trusting this divine power is the source of all goodness in our lives.

Look at how the infinite abundance of the spiritual reality is expressed in nature. One grain of corn will grow a plant with hundreds of grains on it. Every tree has thousands of leaves, every bush, many flowers. Every seed planted, when it comes to maturity, gives us ten or a hundred seeds. Everywhere you look there is more than enough, and sadly the human race is the only expression of Source that seems to negate that abundance. We are also the only expression that has been given free will to choose what we think and do. We must consider the possibility that perhaps we are using our free will in reverse of how it was meant to be used.

All nature, not having free will, falls under the spiritual laws of harmony, cooperation, and abundance. Source has given us free will so we can consciously choose alignment with spiritual laws, but when we choose differently, we fall under the material law of duality, and therefore into the possibility of lack and limitation.

In contrast with the material world we see, the spiritual world is perfect, changeless, eternal, and invisible, so this is where we have some difficulty in considering it real. We so much rely on what we see, hear, or touch to make it real. Thankfully, the Universe is so set up that the outcomes of our choices show very precisely the degree of our alignment with either Source or materiality. The worse your life seems to be, the lower on the scale of frequency you are. And the only way to better your life is not through seeking more money, better health care, or a divorce so you can find a better partner, but primarily through raising your frequency, tuning in to the frequency of Source. Once this has been taken care of, your attention can turn to whatever else would be helpful in the material world.

If there is anything you don't like in the way things are, you must start thinking different thoughts, feeling different feelings, and finally, doing things differently; because one of the definitions of insanity is to keep doing the same things and expecting a different outcome. It does seem as though we are all insane, doing the same things day after day and year after year expecting things to get better. There is hope nevertheless; the Universe always brings up another situation where this time, we can make a better choice. Ultimately, if we are willing to learn, bad choices lead us into making better ones, and good choices into an amazing life.

Trust in the Divine Mind More Than in the Ego-Mind

Unless you trust in that divine source, unless you know it's the fountain from which everything springs, you start getting into problems of all kinds because you don't have the big picture Spirit has of what life is about. A little child trusts and obeys its parents; however, when the child gets to be seven or eight, they think they know better and start getting into all kinds of scrapes until the resulting discomfort or pain makes them search for another less painful way of doing things.

Your ego-mind was given for your protection, so you could survive in this physical world. It operates on the level of materiality, cannot see the vastness of the spiritual world, and is therefore very limited. The ego-mind was given so you could protect yourself from the dangers that were lurking in the first days of humanity on this planet. You could have been devoured by a saber-toothed tiger, or trampled by a mammoth. These were real dangers that could have threatened the survival of the human race, and the ego-mind has done a really good job of protecting us–the race has survived and that kind of danger is no longer a concern, at least not on a daily basis.

But the mind is still there on the lookout, and if there is nothing in the present moment causing you stress, then the mind starts to rehash things that happened in the past and projects them into the future so you can guard yourself from them ever happening again. In one word, your ego-mind is always on the lookout to see that you are safe, protected, and secure. That is its job. It's hardly ever in a peaceful place of just *being*. We can be grateful for having it, and appreciate its usefulness in material life. When it comes to looking after the body, or learning the skills necessary to not only survive but also thrive, it's invaluable.

Now, however, unless you take control of the ego, it's stopping your evolution into a higher spiritual reality. The way life seems to unfold tells you whether your thoughts are mainly in the higher register of knowing that the one power is the source of everything in your life, or in the ego register of believing the things you want are out there in the world. Do you believe that the money you need comes from your boss, your investments, the government, or your partner? If you do, it spells disaster if you lose your job or Wall Street crashes. In your consciousness, you must know everything comes *from* Source, but comes *through* your boss or whoever else. Source provided the abundance to your boss who in turn provides you with some of it. Should you lose your job, Source has infinite ways to provide for your well-being, and when you hold that consciousness, instead of sinking into despair, you start looking for other opportunities. It's a question of consciousness first.

You must become aware you are not your ego, and have evolved to a place where you possess the discernment necessary to know when to listen to your ego, and when to show a higher level of understanding.

When your five-year-old wants to drive your car, do you let him? He's seen you turning the steering wheel and thinks he knows everything about driving a car. Does he, really? You let him pretend he's driving for a little while, let him turn the wheel this way and that, but that's where it stops. Then you take him out of the driver's seat, put him in the back with a seatbelt that will keep him there, and don't pay any attention to his kicking and screaming while you take control and drive the car out on the road.

Your ego is just like that five-year-old thinking he knows everything, and you the parent are like the Spirit that has access to a higher level of knowledge and understanding. You need only turn to that Source, knowing you are an integral part of it, and listen to its guidance. You do not let your ego decide your course of action, however much it kicks, screams, and pleads for your attention.

The ego cannot understand that Real power cannot be increased or diminished–it just is. Real power is not power over some other power–simply, no power exists other than it. Since the ego's nature is powerlessness, it cannot be powerful at the same time. So it reaches out for temporal power over situations it doesn't like, but will never permanently change a situation. Permanence is an attribute of the Spirit. Another similar situation to fight will show up again and again, until the ego surrenders its perceived control to a higher order and recognizes the one power. As you step outside your ego and observe it from a distance–as you create that gap–you can start having an awareness of what Spirit is, and where Real power is.

But you don't get rid of the ego, as has often been taught–it's impossible to continue living a normal human life without it. You simply no longer let it indiscriminately rule your life. You take the time needed to consciously decide how to react to an event or situation. Respond from a place of knowing who you really are, not from the ego perspective. You get to decide your response.

If you still the mind, remember you are Spirit, and as such already have the love, harmony, validation, safety, security, and abundance of every good thing, then you don't need to get it from outside. You have it all, inside, as a feeling of wholeness and completeness that is beyond words. I believe it can descend on you spontaneously, when you simply cannot make sense of a present reality. Then your mind just stops and you find yourself in a place of peace, calm, and tranquility; there is no meaning to anything, things just are.

There Are No Needs When Centered in the Divine Mind

I know what not having needs feels like because I had that experience when I was about twelve years old, in an American military barracks somewhere in Germany. We were refugees, illegally leaving Poland after WWII and the Russian invasion, leaving most of our family and everything we possessed behind. We had spent days hiding in a truck, passing innumerable checkpoints between the Russian, British, and American zones, at each of which we could have been found and sent back.

Reaching the American zone meant safety at last, but all I could feel was numbness, despair, and emptiness. I had lost my known world and couldn't make sense of the days spent hiding under dirty blankets and behind crates, afraid to sneeze or even breathe when soldiers were checking the contents, afraid of nights in the trucks or in abandoned hospitals where I slept on the floor after one look at the mattresses, stained and stiff with dried blood. And now I couldn't make sense of the barracks with two rows of camp beds.

While sitting on my bed, I saw, as in a dream, the GIs coming in with armfuls of stuff–candy and chocolate and things I'd never seen. I was looking, but it didn't mean anything. One of them squatted down beside me to put all the stuff he'd brought on the bed, and when I heard him talk, I didn't understand a word. I realized I had lost contact even with language, lost contact with the outside world, with everything. That was the last straw: my mind stopped, and I burst into tears. I wasn't sad or upset. I had no feelings; tears seemed to just come. I was looking at my surroundings and what was on the camp bed and the GI without knowing who or what anything was and the only reality was I–not the "I" on the bed, but the "I" inside of me. Here, my tears stopped and peace flooded over me. This "I" was total peace; it didn't want or need anything. It just was, and it was enough. When the GI left, I took the stuff on my bed and gave it all away.

I was OK. I needed nothing.

When we are really in the present moment, in the NOW, with no thoughts about where we are or what we are seeing, and when there is no past and no future, we have effectively stopped our egoic mind and can be totally peaceful and content. At the time, I didn't realize what this feeling was, but now I know it was my first experience of there being two of me, one physical and one internal–I had no word for "spiritual" then–and the internal one was what really mattered. That moment passed and other challenges appeared. There was no follow-up on my glimpse of something in me that was greater than anything else until much later in life.

That one great power is present in all of us, whether or not we're conscious of it, and expresses as everything we see, whether it's as sentient, or what we call non-sentient beings or things. Everything is an expression of that one Source, one energy that underlies all visible expression, connects everything to everything else. Just as when you see a field of sage in the desert–small, separate bushes that stretch as far as the horizon, a sea of grayish-yellow plants–you can walk between them, not realizing that underground they have just one root system from which every so often springs a new

THE ONE GREAT POWER: DISCOVERING AND ACCESSING IT

plant. You can't dig up just one bush with all its roots. You have to actually cut the root system that connects it to all the other plants.

Our divinity is our underlying root system, connecting all visible expressions of it, seemingly miles and even worlds apart. We are all connected to Source, and therefore to each other. Just like the Pando, a grove of aspen in Utah having one massive root system, we survive the climatic changes and forest fires of our lives thanks to the connection with our root system, Spirit. We tend to believe we get our supply and security from the visible people, jobs, or corporations surrounding us, but don't stop to think they also get their supply from that one Source.

When you rely on your job or investments and think they are the source of your income, forgetting the Real Source is beyond that apparent temporal source, then losing that job or that partner or the investments seems a disaster. But as soon as you remember that the Real Source has an infinite number of ways through which to provide for your well-being, you already feel better. You trust Spirit will reveal a new channel, keep your eyes open for new possibilities, and take the action that feels right. In your consciousness, you must know that the first and only source of your good, even if it appears to come from other people, is always the power of Sprit. It's never a consciousness of "God looks after me, I will rest in God," then doing nothing; some input from you is always required because God does not act in a vacuum, but *through* some visible means.

You probably heard the story, whether true or not, of a flooded village where police helped evacuate families to safety. Passing the house of the village minister, they called to him to join them. But he shouted back, "God will be my salvation!" and stayed where he was. As the water kept rising, the minister climbed higher to the second floor. More boats passed with people calling to him, but the minister said that he trusted in the mercy of God and would wait for God to save him. Finally, he had to retreat to the roof of his house. The last boat of rescuers came by, and there would not be another chance for the minister; but he still insisted: "I trust in God, I am His servant, He will save me. Go on your way!" So they went on their way. Now there was no one left in the village except the minister. As a last try, a helicopter was sent to pick him up, but he still refused to go; he had always believed in God and in the Scriptures, where it was said that God looked after the righteous. So the helicopter left too, and the water was now so high it almost covered the roof. There was no help in sight. And so despairingly he cried out, "God, where is the help that You have promised to all who trusted and believed in You?" Then he heard God's voice: "My son, I sent you many boats, and even a helicopter, but you refused My help. There is nothing more I can do!"

You are an expression of God in physicality; you must know it and live it so your soul's agenda can be physically expressed. It's up to you to recognize the hand of Spirit in everything that happens and recognize it must be for your highest good, even if you can't see why or how right now. That recognition alone will set you in the right direction, where you would look for the opportunity to grow because of the event.

Review of chapter 1:
- ⬥ There is only one power: it's everywhere; therefore, it must be where you are.
- ⬥ When you think you are separate from Spirit, you cannot access its power.
- ⬥ But when you know you are the point where Spirit expresses, no one and nothing can have power over you.

CHAPTER 2

THE POWER WITHIN: RECLAIMING YOUR RESPONSIBILITY

Sitting in the train taking me to the airport at 5 a.m., I was feeling happy about leaving the snowstorm at home for sunny California. Happy about the workshop I would be attending and being able to keep up with my commitments through my computer.

With that, my heart stopped: all I could say was, "Oh my God!" over and over. I had forgotten my computer! And I really needed it. Thoughts swirled through my mind: teleconferences I was supposed to attend; clients I could not contact—no addresses, no phone numbers; fifty-plus emails a day piling up that I would have to wade through when I got back . . . . Each thought just triggered another, worse than before. Apart from going back for the computer and missing my plane, there was nothing I could do.

That was not an option.

It took no more than a minute, and I remembered my practice. Change your thoughts! Taking a deep breath, I hit the "pause" button in my brain and looked at the facts. No computer and a plane to the States in two hours. Inconvenient, upsetting, but there are worse things in life. What's the opportunity in this? What's the hidden possibility? What's the potential benefit or gift?

Even without seeing any gifts as yet, just switching my thoughts to possible benefits, I had recovered some peace of mind; my heart started beating again. One obvious benefit, my case would be lighter! I could have a real holiday for a few days without any business at all and deal with upset people when I got back. Intellectually, I knew every situation is always for my ultimate benefit, though right then it certainly didn't feel that way—so I breathed, relaxed, and waited for the benefits to appear.

Within five minutes of discovering the "disaster," I was feeling peaceful even though the situation hadn't changed at all—and wouldn't change, because facts are facts. I had made the decision to catch that plane without having my computer, and then chose to be accepting and peaceful rather than upset and angry with myself. That activated more ability to see other outcomes. I had a peaceful flight listening to uplifting conferences on my iPad; once in the States, I found a technical guru to configure my iPad to connect to the Internet and receive emails—something I had never done, since I only used it as a library. As a result, I became more adept and skilled at using other means than my computer. I got to know people I would never have met otherwise, and I ended up with more, rather than with less; more of me had come out.

The Vision of Source Is the True Vision of the World

You can only access the power that is within you when you become aware that you are not your name, your body, your profession, or any of your usual identifications. Instead, you are a spiritual being expressing in the world of duality which uses your mind and body in order to experience sensations. The spiritual world is invisible, infinite, omnipresent, and omnipotent, and projects this realm of manifestation, which you call your reality. Your soul lives in the perfect spiritual Reality, but when that comes through your human mind, it gets distorted out of its perfection and becomes what you see with the physical senses. It's just a picture, a limited and inaccurate representation of the original perfection. Just as when you take a photo of a flower through a lens that is dirty or cracked or has a filter on it, the flower will come out distorted, fuzzy, and the color not quite the same.

We have all had experiences where an event we witnessed was later described by another person who also witnessed it, and what they described was very different from our perception. They are not lying; it's just that they saw the event through the filters in their mind, while we saw it through the filters in ours. The well-known spiritual teacher Michael Beckwith summed it up beautifully when he said, "We do not describe what we see; we see what we describe."[1]

When you have really internalized what we discussed in the first chapter–that there is only one Presence and one Power and that it's everywhere, so it must be where you are and what you are; that every event, whatever it looks like, is also a part of that Presence and Power and infinite good–then there can be no adverse situation. You are the focal point through which that power flows to make your life become what you would like it to be. It's up to you to know this, and use it. It is also up to everyone else to know this, and use that power to make their lives the very best they can.

It's each one's responsibility to get as close as possible to God's vision of the events we see; the more aligned we are with that vision, the fewer problems we encounter and the easier life seems to flow. Said in another way, the higher your overall frequency, the smoother and happier your life becomes. Your only Real power is spiritual because it's infinite and eternal. Your human power always changes; one day you have it, the next you don't. Power in the material sense is power *over* someone or *over* a situation or a condition. Power in the spiritual sense is something completely different. Since Spirit is one, consciousness is one, and all its attributes are one; so power also is one, and there is nothing–no other power–to have power over. Spiritual power, ultimately, is simply identifying that all power flows through you to think and act as the Spirit you know yourself to be. In other words, raise your frequency, your temporal consciousness, closer to that of your soul.

Your temporal consciousness is a part of what can be called collective consciousness, made up of all the beliefs held as true by a great number of people. Often they are false, but they get accepted as true through centuries of repetition. They have been taught and believed–and it is time to really look at your beliefs to see if they still hold true for you.

Change Is Always Possible

You never have to stay a victim of events or circumstances–or in a belief that is no longer true for you–if you don't want to. You can get yourself out of depressing thoughts and unhappiness not by changing a situation, but rather by changing your perception. In the train, after I realized that I had forgotten my computer, it took less than five minutes to shift my perceptions, even though the situation was still the same. Understand that you activate all the latent power of your Spirit through knowing you are that Spirit and responding to the situation in front of you from that place. You do have that power; everyone has, but you must choose to consciously activate it. The code for accessing the power and gifts that are already yours is in aligning your thoughts, words, and actions with what you imagine, in every moment, would be the highest expression of Spirit.

> There is no power outside of you that has power over you.

The implications of this are huge. First, that there is no power outside of you that has power over you. In victim consciousness, you are not aware of having power, so you can't use it. You believe things are done to you; someone else, or you yourself, is always to blame for the situation. Thoughts of "I'm not able . . . I'm not capable . . . I'll lose . . . I can't do . . . I won't have . . ." keep you in separation from the wisdom and power of your divine Self. That's giving

THE POWER WITHIN: RECLAIMING YOUR RESPONSIBILITY

your power away to other people, places, or things–comparable to when John couldn't access the million dollars in his attic until he discovered it was there. Once you recognize your power, it's the end of victimhood. It's the end of the belief that there is power in a bad economy, in corporations, in money, in a health diagnosis. You start realizing that life happens *through* you, not *to* you. Now you are moving from being a victim to taking personal responsibility for your own thoughts, feelings, and actions.

And so in your everyday life, with a little awareness, you get to decide whether the disparaging remark someone made about your work or your cooking is important enough to make you feel upset. You may decide to brush it off and forget about it, or just remember the time when you were showered with compliments on the project you presented. And if you manage to keep that happy thought in mind for ninety seconds, it will trigger another happy thought and another. Notice how you were no longer upset during that time. So you *can* take responsibility for your thoughts and choose only those that serve you.

But what about the really traumatic, dramatic events that happen where there seems to be no way to turn off the mind that keeps revolving around the event and returning to the place of absolute loss with no solution is sight? Remembering Spirit loves you unconditionally and therefore your experience *must* be for your highest good, even if you don't see how, is still the most important practice. But sometimes your mind simply stops on its own, just long enough for you to reach that place of peace and stillness where nothing has meaning anymore. That time in the military barracks, Spirit did that for me; it allowed me to see things without any meaning attached to them. In the normal course of events, this does not happen. You have to engineer it; so what you can do is very consciously change the meaning of a traumatic event to a different one, and keep searching for new meanings–however improbable–it could possibly have. You don't know which of them will manifest, maybe several will. Focus on the ones that feel a little less despairing, less painful. That is Spirit, helping you drop the sad and despondent thoughts so as to bring you back into balance. From there, after a while, you can again restart your life. Once you've reached that place of balance, even if your dark thoughts do return, it is now easier to take control–stop putting a meaning on the situation–and bit by bit regain peace and serenity.

Blaming others for what they did is really easy, but remember that it's never anyone's actions that are responsible for your feelings; it's always your thoughts and emotions *about* those actions that make you feel a certain way. Once you realize it's your own thoughts that make you unhappy and make you feel like a victim, you are motivated to take back your power to see things differently and to consider the event from a higher perspective: the perspective of Spirit, whose agenda is always your spiritual evolution.

Intellectual Knowing Is Not Enough–You Have to Claim It and Feel It

You only need to start claiming and using that power for your life to become what you would like it to be. To claim that power, you first need to change your thinking–which will change your feelings and vibration–to access solutions not seen before and, consequently, to change your actions.

In a world where thoughts and feelings lead to concrete manifestation, action is required to bring thoughts and inventions into materiality. From the time we are born, we are endowed with free will that lets us choose which action to take when. Our whole life is just a series of choices we make all the time. We use our discernment to choose an action that will give the best possible outcome, but sometimes we may not like the outcome of our action. So we think we have made a wrong choice.

THE POWER WITHIN: RECLAIMING YOUR RESPONSIBILITY

It may seem like a wrong choice; yet remember you are not a human being, but rather a Spirit having a human experience, and to Spirit there is no such thing as "wrong." There is just an opportunity to grow in some way or make the decision to act differently next time.

What looks like a wrong choice, because it's painful, may be the right choice from the standpoint of Spirit, because the pain taught us something we needed to learn, such as compassion or better understanding. Sometimes, what looks like the right choice from the human point of view, considering it gives us more money, recognition, or a job, may not be what Spirit wanted because it bypassed a lesson we were supposed to learn, or because we are not yet at a level where we will not misuse the power that job gives us, or misuse the wealth we've been given. Spiritually speaking, when we misuse what we have, we have regressed instead of progressed. So when things don't work out the way we wanted them to, we need to accept that things are exactly what they're supposed to be, because the Universe always works for us, not against us. We don't have to like it, but we do have to acknowledge that everything is for our highest, ultimate good. Based on that principle, we endeavor to recognize the gift, learn the lesson, and align with the perspective of Source.

Your soul incarnated because it wanted to have experiences through the physical body, otherwise it would have stayed a pure spirit in the spiritual world. The spiritual part of the soul remains the same, while the physical part gets developed, and you grow and learn how to manage your life to make it as comfortable as possible. Even as a baby, you learn by experience. Once you've experienced something that results in pain, you know not to do it again.

Born into dense physicality, you gradually forget your spirituality and, as a child, act solely from the human standpoint. As a teenager, you make decisions, take action, and sometimes the outcome is not what you would have liked. That was not a wrong decision, but one where you learned what not to do in a similar situation. The older you get, the more you start to realize there is a part of you that is connected to all the knowledge of the Universe–called intuition. That is communication from your soul, which will always contribute most to your spiritual growth, even if it doesn't immediately give you more money, better health, or the ideal partner. Still, as your relationship with Spirit strengthens and becomes more real, all its attributes can flow into your world when they're no longer stopped by your doubts, fears, or limiting beliefs.

Your soul's perspective is perfection, but it comes through your mind, through all the cultural, parental, and relational filters you have acquired either from parents, teachers, friends, TV programs, or from just life on this planet. The pure vision gets distorted. Similarly, when you take a picture through a dirty or cracked lens, the picture will not reflect the beauty you wanted to immortalize.

Action Must Follow Thought to Be Manifested

If you really knew that your soul's power, beauty, harmony, wisdom, and abundance of every good thing were within you–and are you–then you would discern your soul's undistorted view and would know that whatever your circumstances, you have the capacity to be peaceful and harmonious regardless of conditions. When you are rooted in Spirit, there can be no adverse situation. As the saying goes: "One with God is a majority," but there can be "situations." However, solving a "situation" from the vibrational level of the problem will never be a permanent solution. The essence of that problem will just manifest as another problem. So our level of thinking must rise from the material to the spiritual in order to change what we don't like experiencing. Changing our perception, which changes our frequency, is the first key to a permanent solution.

Then action must follow thought, so the next key is the ability to respond from that expanded place. In the example of forgetting my computer, I first changed my perception of the situation, became

THE POWER WITHIN: RECLAIMING YOUR RESPONSIBILITY

peaceful, accessed new insights on how to proceed, and then searched for people who could help and teach me what I needed to learn. Your response to a situation or an event determines your experience of it, and that comes from your experiences of the past: the feelings you had, your fears regarding the future, behaviors you may have witnessed, or your own behaviors. If you respond from the vibration of your past life, you will keep re-creating similar situations until you decide to have a different, higher response. You have been given free will so you can choose your thoughts and actions, and those determine your experiences.

What does it really mean to say the power to change is where you are and within you? Is it in the ground under your feet or in the air around you? Consider that electricity is everywhere, and you can experience it when touching the metal edge of your car. You get a small shock from static electricity. Now, let's speak at a deeper level. Comparable to electricity, consciousness is everywhere. Since all power is in consciousness (as established in chapter 1), and you have consciousness, it follows that all power is within your own temporal consciousness.

We can use that power just as we use electricity. Until someone had discovered electricity and put in structures to harness it to make it useful, we lived in darkness as soon as the sun set. If a house has the necessary structures for making electricity flow into a light bulb, we will have light. Conversely, the house that is not wired will be in darkness even though there is electricity around it, too. In this same way, we live in darkness, or with problems until we find the structures that will make that power flow through us.

The main structures allowing access to spiritual power are prayer, meditation, and watching the kind of thoughts we habitually have. Prayer is a first step, even though it is usually reduced to asking God for what seems to be missing from your life. When you really understand that God is in you, and is you, you also realize

He already knows what you want, and, like a loving parent, has it ready for you just as soon as you are able to receive it without harm resulting. When your two-year-old insists on grabbing that entrancing lighted candle, do you give it to him? Or do you wait till he's able to receive it without great pain as a result?

As your awareness and comprehension of spiritual values grow, your prayers tend to change, becoming more of a meditation on the nature and perfection of God. Your laundry list of things you want disappears. At those times of prayer and meditation, you are consciously connected through your attention and intention. But thoughts are also very important, because from them stem our feelings, and from those stem our behaviors. During the rest of the day, when not in meditation, are your habitual thoughts congruent with the peace, harmony, and love of Spirit, or are they in the register of defensiveness, frustration, anger, guilt, or blame? Watch, and as soon as you're aware of negativity, reverse the trend of your thought. Are we mostly smiling or frowning? Every joyous, happy, or harmonious feeling raises our vibration and connects us with the wisdom, genius, and inspiration from Spirit, allowing us to rise above the frequency of the problem to where solutions are found.

> Every joyous, happy, or harmonious feeling raises our vibration and connects us with the wisdom, genius, and inspiration from Spirit.

Individual Consciousness vs. Collective Consciousness

Your individual consciousness is part of the collective consciousness made of beliefs held as true by humanity at large. Those beliefs, however, are not necessarily true and many have been

THE POWER WITHIN: RECLAIMING YOUR RESPONSIBILITY

changed over the years. For example, look at the belief we had in the Middle Ages that the earth was a flat disk. It seems laughable now, but it was held as true in many cultures, including ancient Greece, and also China until the seventeenth century.

Recall Galileo, the sixteenth century mathematician and astronomer, who adopted and championed Copernicus's theory of the sun being the center of our solar system. The Roman Inquisition refused to accept this notion. Galileo was tried and found guilty of heresy, spending the rest of his life under house arrest. It took time to change that belief, but eventually it became the new truth.

So, changing an individual consciousness can shatter a collective false belief; as proof accumulates, and a critical mass is reached, the false belief just disappears. Consider the many beliefs, big or small, that are continually being challenged and abandoned. Once Roger Bannister shattered the belief that no one could run a mile in under four minutes, people are now regularly breaking that record.

Look closely at your own beliefs of who you are, what you can do, who you can become, to see whether they are true in the light of the belief that you are a pure, undistorted expression of Source. "What you think, you become" is a well-known quote. A belief is just a thought held many times over, so make sure your thoughts and beliefs expand you rather than diminish you.

Your individual belief will mold your experience, regardless of the collective belief that may be different. Imagine Columbus taking with him a friend who believed the earth was flat. Neither of them would have fallen off the edge of the world, but the friend, willing to accompany Columbus, would have had a very fearful and uncomfortable ride, while Columbus would have had a peaceful and happy one. You don't change truth by your belief or disbelief; instead, you change your experience. The friend was willing to attempt something new in spite of his disbelief–and the truth would manifest for him the same as for Columbus. If you are willing to put a new belief to the test, the truth will also manifest for you.

Be willing to believe the power of Divinity is where you are—because it's everywhere and in everything that surrounds you; you tune in to it through your awareness and love.

Energy, another word for Spirit or Divinity, is everywhere. But to experience its benefits, you have to first know it, and then build structures to experience its effects in your life. You must become aligned with the frequency of your Spirit. Derek Rydall gives the example of radio waves in the atmosphere everywhere, playing music and giving information of every kind, but unless you have a receiver, such as a radio, you can't hear any of it. And the radio has to have a dial so you can choose what station, which broadcast to listen to, by tuning in to that specific frequency. If you don't know where the station you want might be, you try them all one by one until you find the music you want, and then stay on that frequency. There are many stations with information or music you don't want—and if you happen to tune in to one of those, all you have to do is turn the dial until you find what you like.

When it comes to tuning ourselves to the frequency of Spirit, we are now talking about a deeper level than radio waves, which have to have some material structure in order for us to access and use them. That deeper level is called consciousness, and your dial to get to the station you want is choosing where to put your attention. Consciousness is one, as we've seen before, and is all power; you are consciousness and therefore part of its power. That means all power is within you, exactly where you are, and you can tune in to the wholeness of it through directing your attention to the things, events, and situations you like and want.

When you focus on frequencies generated by human beings, carrying false and limiting beliefs of lack, disease, anger, fear, and shame, among many others, and let your thoughts dwell on the disturbing and unwanted appearances, it's like tuning your TV to the movie that upsets you. Do you stay there, or do you change your channel?

THE POWER WITHIN: RECLAIMING YOUR RESPONSIBILITY

To change your channel, you have been given free will–the dial on a radio–so you can access the frequencies you want to listen to and live in. You are aware of both the spiritual and the human qualities of the world where you live, and must use your free will to align with one or the other through thoughts, feelings, and actions. You activate what you most desire, whether it's love, support, compassion, or validation, by knowing you spiritually already have it, since you are part of the One Consciousness that has it all. But to bring them into your physical world, you must first give out those qualities to others so they can be reflected back. You become truly aware that everything you could possibly need is within, just waiting to be activated and brought into physicality through you.

Consciousness Is Life and Life Is Source Energy

All the great scriptures and great teachers have told us that. Buddha was teaching his followers that the power is within them. We read in the Bible, "Behold, the dwelling place of God is with man." (Revelation 21:3) God told Moses, when facing the burning bush that was not being consumed, "Do not come any closer. Take off your sandals, for you are standing on holy ground." (Exodus 3:5) This essentially means that Moses, a human being embodying the Spirit of God, was making the ground he was standing on sacred. Jesus was teaching the same thing when He said, "The kingdom of God is within you." (Luke 17:21) And in modern times, quantum physics is proving the spiritual knowledge of ancient teachings through the "observer effect": that we are part of a quantum field, made of pure consciousness and information, where nothing happens until we observe it. The power of our attention changes physics. Our consciousness through our attention activates a power, makes particles behave differently than when they are not observed.

Your consciousness is the animating principle of your body; without it, the body can no longer move or see or hear. The Real

You interpenetrates your body and mind to make it act, but it is also beyond the body, and is the one Consciousness. Every cell in your body has a certain level of consciousness, but you can lose your foot, arm, or other parts of your body without it necessarily affecting the power your consciousness has to triumph over all material obstacles that seemingly stand in your way. How they affect you is your choice.

One example of this is the life of Nick Vujicic, an Australian born without arms or legs. It would seem that a life of total dependence on others, loneliness, and depression awaited him; however, he overcame all his challenges, started speaking to audiences at the age of nineteen to share his story, and delivered a message of hope and possibility of living a fulfilled life, regardless of the challenges anyone has. He is married, is an author, an actor, a musician, paints and swims, and he freely admits it is the power of Spirit within that has allowed him to rise out of the depression of his early years and his feeling of being different and alone. He lives a more fulfilled and happier life than many whose challenges are minuscule by comparison.

Another well-known example is that of Nelson Mandela, imprisoned for his political views for twenty-seven years. The hardships he endured, even refusing to be liberated so he could stay coherent with his convictions and his nonviolent struggle against apartheid, did not break his spirit, did not make him bitter or resentful. He came out of the ordeal stronger, owning the power he knew he had. And when finally released, Mandela became the President of South Africa and officially ended apartheid, something he had struggled for all his life.

Every day throughout his twenty-seven years of imprisonment, Mandela reportedly read the poem "Invictus," meaning undefeated, by William Ernest Henley. He said it helped him deepen his understanding and fully own the power of his soul.

THE POWER WITHIN: RECLAIMING YOUR RESPONSIBILITY

Out of the night that covers me,
Black as the pit from pole to pole,
I thank whatever gods may be
For my unconquerable soul.

In the fell clutch of circumstance
I have not winced nor cried aloud
Under the bludgeonings of chance
My head is bloody, but unbowed.

Beyond this place of wrath and tears
Looms but the Horror of the shade,
And yet the menace of the years
Finds and shall find me unafraid.

It matters not how strait the gate,
How charged with punishments the scroll,
I am the master of my fate:
I am the captain of my soul.[2]

This "I" the poem refers to that is unafraid of circumstances, unafraid of the horrors, the darkness, and the punishments life presents is the same "I" that Moses experienced in the revelation of the burning bush, hearing the words "I AM that I AM." (Exodus 3:14) It's the same "I" Jesus declared when he said, "I AM the Way, the Truth and the Life." (John 14:6) These same words read backward reveal an additional meaning: "The Life and the Truth, the way I AM." In this interpretation, we are that Light and Truth exactly as we are now; we are the full activity of God expressed through us. Life and Light, used spiritually, are synonymous.

I AM is the name of God, so whatever quality you put after the words I AM is Spirit declaring itself as that.

"I AM peace."
"I AM joy."
"I AM harmony, wisdom, health, wealth, abundance . . . ."

Let's be very conscious of the words that we put after the declaration of "I AM" so that they reflect only the Truth of your Being. When you say I am sick, I am poor, or I am unhappy, you are stating an untruth in respect to your Divinity, which cannot be sick, poor, or unhappy. You are reversing the principle of life, which is all perfection, and creating a situation that in Reality cannot exist. But it does or will exist *in your experience*, since that is what you, as co-creator, have decreed. Declaring what you want with the full realization that the "I" within you is the Spirit that is speaking, and that Spirit is all-powerful, you cannot fail to manifest the desires that are in alignment with those of Spirit.

Shift Your Perceptions

I was about ten when I first was shown this truth. For the world, it was the end of WWII, but for me, the beginning of another invasion. The night the Germans left, there was palpable silence in the streets, a feeling of lightness like a window being opened on a sunny spring morning, but also an apprehensive expectancy. The Russians were coming. I went down to the river to watch. The bridge had been blown up, so they couldn't get to me. I felt safe.

I heard them first, the shooting, the shouts, the pounding of hooves. Then a long line of horse-drawn carts appeared on the opposite bank, filled with bearded figures in black furs and bearskins, cracking long whips, yelling wildly and shooting. It was just like the pictures in my history book of the fourteenth century Tartar invasions. My heart started pounding, but curiosity kept me there. They stopped, right opposite to me. Jumping off the carts, unloading canoes to lay a pontoon bridge at what seemed lightning speed, running along the planks to lay the next one, and the next . . . . They were

THE POWER WITHIN: RECLAIMING YOUR RESPONSIBILITY

now more than halfway across the river, and I could clearly see their bearded faces. One of them straightened up and looked right at me, the fur on his face indistinguishable from the fur bearskin on his head. His wild eyes and his expression froze me. I couldn't move, couldn't look away. He was so close I realized he would be up on the bank in no time at all, and a wave of fear washed over me. I was sure he could hear my heart pounding—and thoughts raced through my head. Holding his eyes would stop him . . . I couldn't stay like that forever . . . if I turned he'd come after me. The fear was overwhelming. With a huge effort I looked away—and never stopped running till I got home, feeling all of them right behind me. They were coming. It seemed like all the heaviness and apprehensiveness of the previous seven years of war was back. Breathing was difficult.

That night, hearing shouting, wild singing, and seeing the red glow of fires reflected in the window, I quietly got out of bed and sat to watch. I was up on the second floor, high above the square. Black figures in shaggy furs were dragging chairs, tables, and furniture from neighboring houses to keep the fires going. Others were weaving about holding bottles of vodka and singing drunken songs; shooting and the tinkle of breaking glass added to the confusion. Guns were neatly stacked close to the fires and easily accessible.

The situation was much worse than this morning, houses being looted, fires in the square, drunken brawls, but I was no longer at that level—I could look from a much higher place where the turmoil down below could no longer affect me. Watching everything from a different perspective, I was at peace. Nothing could reach me here—not like earlier, when I was at the level of the problem.

Potentially, the situation was worse than that morning, but strangely enough, I felt a sense of tranquility up on the second floor. From a higher vantage point—I was safe, even interested. They couldn't get me where I was.

Perspective makes all the difference.

Our perception of what a situation is can easily shift, since what is will appear much less threatening from a higher perspective. Even if you don't fully understand it as yet, you can feel that the consciousness of the "I AM" within you is the only power that can change your experiences.

Since you have desires, it means you are not completely satisfied with the way things are, and, perhaps until now, your mindset was in victimhood. Your perception is *All these things are happening to me; I never wanted this disease; I never asked to be fired from my job. It's the fault of the economy, of my boss, or the government. I really love my partner, why are they treating me this way?* This is called giving away your power to people, circumstances, or situations.

But now you have come to realize the "I" within you, your consciousness, has power, and you can activate it through your thoughts, perceptions, and intentions—all those invisible processes that have been used by people like Nelson Mandela and Nick Vujicic to lift them out of victimhood and not bow to circumstances they could not change. The only change they could make was a change in their own thoughts and perceptions, and even if it took years, in the end, their lives changed. In the case of Mandela, his actual physical circumstances changed—he was released from prison, became president, and passed the laws abolishing apartheid. In the case of Vujicic, his physical circumstances never changed, but through identifying more with his Spirit than with his body, he lives a happy and fulfilled life, helping others rise above their various handicaps. So identifying more with Spirit than with materiality always brings a change for the better—but that is different for everyone, in accordance with their individual calling.

You have the exact same Spirit within you that they had—or have—that incarnated in order to express itself through you. Where and to whom you were born, all the circumstances of your life, all the situations you've been faced with are contributing to making you the most perfect expression of your soul exactly where you are now. It only needs first for you to become aware, and then to integrate, to own the knowledge that "I am the master of my fate: I am the captain of my soul."[3]

So the power to change starts with changing the perception of who you are. The power is in that invisible "I" that I AM, which is your soul, not in the "I" of your personality, the physical, mental, and emotional construct called ego. The ego tries to change things in the visible world; however, since it does not have the expanded view the soul has, it doesn't really know which conditions are better for your ultimate good. It chooses conditions that satisfy material desires, yet somehow those are never enough to satisfy you in the long run. They may please you for a time, but then you always end up wanting more or better things.

You Are a Spirit, Not a Physical Body

Notice how your life has been unfolding: when you were a child, the material things of life were the only important ones. And that was perfect; you came from a spiritual world into a material world and had to learn how things work in this different dimension and how to interact with others, so you could have a life without too many upsets or hurts, whether physical, mental, or emotional. And you managed; you knew how to live a child's life.

Then as your body developed, other needs became apparent. You now wanted to choose your clothes, become better than others in football or tennis, go to college or learn a trade. You dreamed of a high salary, an interesting job, the ideal partner, a house, some beautiful kids. That's all perfect, and you achieve some of that, if not all. But once you've got it, you find that you need a better job, a bigger salary, or a larger house. You achieve that again, and then continue the cycle with a more responsible job, a better salary, or another partner. It's never enough, for you are still unfulfilled and realize material things don't bring you the permanent joy and happiness you want, so you start searching outside the material, in the spiritual realm.

Because you are Spirit, not a physical body, physical things will never fully satisfy you. You have tried getting material things for years, and it has proved not enough. You can, of course, stay in material perceptions, and that is OK, too. Spirit has given you free will to choose whatever you want and always honors your choice. Life will keep happening, and your experiences will indicate whether you have made a choice more, or less, aligned with spiritual laws.

If you have seen that living a purely material life is not working for you, then you start to expand your area of search for happiness beyond what you have known so far. What lies underneath all the visible achievements and trappings of life is Spirit, from which springs all you think you are. Let me say that again, because it's so important: all you think you are comes from Spirit. You have not been using its full power for lack of awareness that it's even here, let alone that it's your very life.

You have been becoming more aware of your Spirit as we've been progressing, and now, in order to use the power dormant within you, it's necessary to take responsibility. You have learned to take responsibility in your material life, but now a deeper aspect of responsibility appears: your "response-ability" to events and situations must shift if you are not totally happy and fulfilled in spite of material achievements. Now your responses must come from your soul; you feel there must be more to life than just money, a house, a boat, and a partner. Those are really nice to have, but you will never feel fully satisfied until you focus on spiritual values and bring those values into the world through service to others in whatever way you are most suited. Whether it's through painting, teaching, or music, or whether you are a plumber, mechanic, or the CEO of a company, bring your Spirit through everything you do to fulfill your purpose.

THE POWER WITHIN: RECLAIMING YOUR RESPONSIBILITY

Whatever shows up in your life, especially the unwanted things, is only there so that you can consciously choose a higher response from a place of love for all energy and from connection with the power of your Spirit, rather than a reaction from the ego which is feeling hurt or disrespected. A higher response can only be activated through stopping all judgments about people or situations facing you, no matter how they might appear. Start looking for the opportunity within them for your spiritual evolution. Just that in itself is already a higher response that will open up more possibilities for a change.

For example, a situation we often face is dealing with all those drivers on the freeway who should have their licenses taken away! And so, as you get cut off in traffic, you can choose:

- ❖ to react, get angry, and shake your fist at the offender who doesn't even see you, or
- ❖ to realize they had almost missed their exit, and let the incident go.

The first choice will leave you with the experience of feeling upset and resentful. Your second choice will leave you feeling peaceful and pleased that there was no accident. Perhaps, you may even be thankful for your own quick reaction, which is of course a response from your Spirit.

We Are Creators with Responsibility

Acting from your place of power makes you the creator of your life. Too often, taking responsibility is construed as blaming yourself: it's my fault; I'm responsible for this mess. This leads to shame and being a victim again. Nothing is your fault; your actions stem from the knowledge you have at any given moment. You do the best you know how, and if the outcome is not what you expected, you learn from the experience and act from a higher perception next time.

Remember that you were born into collective false beliefs, so you only have partial information; as life progresses, you adjust your ideas, abandon some beliefs, and create new ones that serve you better. Since at your core you are Spirit, choosing behaviors that reflect spiritual values will give you the best experiences.

Life keeps presenting you with situations, and taking responsibility is still the key element. You have shifted to recognizing there must be more to life than just getting a bigger house or a better partner, and you are searching for responses that come from your soul, the spiritual values. Whatever you're facing is only there so you can choose a higher response than in the past.

I can think of several instances in my job when a colleague, and once even my boss, had issues with the way I was doing things. I always justified myself: it wasn't my fault, it was this or that circumstance. It started with little inconsequential things, but they grew more serious each time, culminating when an angry and abusive colleague stormed into my office. I was speechless. Just listened, gradually becoming aware this had nothing to do with me. When he ran out of breath, I very quietly said, "I am so sorry you are having a bad day." There was no anger in me, no justifying anything; I felt really sorry for him. He just looked at me and stormed out without another word. I don't know where that came from, for it wasn't a planned, conscious response. It surprised me as much as it surprised him.

I never again had any issues with anyone in the office. Of course problems arose, they always do, but never with any angry or upsetting remarks. Only much later I realized that in that particular moment I was able to give a higher response from a place of compassion and understanding. I hadn't consciously chosen that response; it came directly as a gift from Spirit, but I never forgot it. That time, my soul acted through me. Yet how do we use that power when faced with much bigger and more serious issues, like disease, fear, or loss?

THE POWER WITHIN: RECLAIMING YOUR RESPONSIBILITY

I would invite you to take a moment and bring to mind any issue you currently have. What has been your internal–or perhaps even external–response to that issue? Is it worry, anxiety, upset, or anger? Instead, identify with your all-powerful, all-allowing soul: what would be its response to that situation? And if right now you can find no redeeming grace in the situation at all, consider that the mere fact of turning your attention to Spirit has created a gap between you and your problem. Your anxiety has lifted a little. Only after connecting with Spirit, you start to materially improve the situation; and the more you do that, the easier it will become to shift it. Your soul only sees the positive aspects; just align with its perspective, even if you don't know what it is. "Divine Spirit, I don't know how this is for my highest good, but I do know it must be; so I sincerely thank you for this gift!"

To Access the Power of Spirit, Structures Are Necessary

You can awaken the dormant power of your soul by building structures to harness it, just as electricity is harnessed for light or making toast. The main structures for making Divinity apparent and practical in your life are prayer, meditation, and carefully watching your habitual thoughts. Are they joyful, loving, and compassionate, or resentful, sad, and fearful? Happy, harmonious thoughts raise your vibration closer to that of Spirit where no problems exist, while trying to resolve a problem from a place of anger or fear will never permanently solve it. Temporarily, things might seem to get better; but the essence of that problem will only flare up in some other part of your life. As Einstein said: "We cannot solve our problems with the same level of thinking that created them."[4]

Every problem lives at its own specific vibration, and they are all called "negative" or "unwanted." As long as you feel fearful, doubtful, angry, disrespected, or unworthy, negativity will be your experience. Once you raise your vibration out of that frequency into acceptance and see a new opportunity, the outcomes will be of a much higher order. Sometimes, even the simple acknowledgement of a situation may shift it. Your reaction usually comes from your remembrance of the past or fears for the future. But you can choose to have different thoughts.

I remember the story of a man whose chain saw slipped and cut his thigh almost to the bone. His first thought was, *Thank God it stopped there and I still have my leg!* He just kept having positive thoughts while in hospital and his recovery was spectacular, according to the medical staff.

Really understand that you activate whatever quality you want through your awareness. Awareness is in the invisible realm of pure energy that is colored by our human experiences, so the pure qualities of Source, as they come through a human mind, are colored or distorted out of their original form. Your job, as a human being, is to bring those qualities down into the visible, manifested world in the best way you know how, and that will be different for every person. It starts with just an intellectual awareness that you do have whatever you need to fulfill your deepest desires because Spirit contains all the qualities required to manifest them, and you are your Spirit.

Manifestation in the physical world requires action, and you must provide that. Remember: everything happens *through* you, not *to* you. You create your experience of events by your thoughts and feelings about them. You are never a victim, unless you choose to be. So take full responsibility for your perspective of any situation. Align your thoughts with what you imagine would be the response of Divinity, before the intruding thoughts of "How can I . . . There's no money in this . . . I'm not good enough . . . I'll lose . . . I won't get . . ."

What would have been the response of my Divinity when I discovered I had forgotten my computer? Surely: "No big deal, I will find other ways and everything will be OK!" And in fact, everything was OK. Take a moment to imagine the response of Divinity in a situation that is facing you right now.

Everything always works out; maybe not in the ways you wanted it, but always in ways it is supposed to work out for your ultimate good. You don't have to like it; that's being honest with yourself and your feelings. Give yourself permission to dislike the occurrence, to hate it even; you have the right to feel any emotion that comes up in that moment. Don't act it out on the outside, just give yourself permission to feel whatever you are feeling about the situation on the inside. And what you will find is that the feeling dissolves, melts, and disappears. As soon as you have permission to do something, resistance is gone. When you harbor hate and resentment, you think that's unspiritual: *I should have better feelings.* That's self-judgment. However, if you allow those feelings, there is no self-judgment because the harmony of your Spirit automatically shows up and dissolves the war between what is and what you think should be. You realize that only by loving the energy that underlies all its various aspects, and allowing them space to be, you will change your perception. Then stand in your true power and choose a response from a place of compassion and understanding, without being a doormat.

The World Outside Reflects Our Vision of It

The world you see outside is a mirror of your internal landscape. When you look in a mirror and don't like the way your hair looks, do you try and change the image in the mirror? Or do you change your hairdo, which will then reflect back to you another image? When you transpose that example to a deeper level, you will start asking different questions, start having a different perspective. What other explanation could there be for the behavior you're seeing in people around you? Is it possible that it has nothing to do with you?

Perhaps they are in so much pain from some past event in their own life that they indiscriminately lash out at whoever reminds them of it? By choosing to look at angry, mean, or hateful characters as people who are in so much pain they're not even aware of the pain they're inflicting on others, you can let go of judgments. By becoming aware of their pain you activate compassion. And choosing to see another's pain versus judging their behavior is the highest form of forgiveness. That's the end of any resentment, grudge, or judgment you may have. Love, in the highest sense of the word, will automatically come up in its place.

On the energetic level, that's all that needs to be done, and sometimes that is enough. But since we live in a material and concrete world, often it is also necessary to take action. Once you are clear on the energetic level, your actions will be dictated by your own discernment and what your intuition guides you to do, rather than by anger or resentment. Even then, sometimes, the outcome is not what you expected, and you think you've made a wrong choice.

On the human level of experience, what you have chosen to do may look like a wrong choice; you may have lost some money, or your partner got really upset with you. Realize that "wrong" is a judgment, when really an event is an opportunity to make a choice from a different consciousness than you were in a week, an hour, or a year ago. Acknowledge things are as they are for your highest good even when you don't like them, and that in itself evolves you to a level of understanding you did not have in your last challenge. Every experience is welcomed by the soul. It incarnated to have experiences, and your best course of action is the one that contributes most to your spiritual growth, not the one that will give you material comfort. As your relationship with Spirit strengthens and becomes more real, its attributes can more easily flow into your world since they are no longer stopped by your doubts and fears.

Those doubts, fears, and false beliefs are like the kinks in a garden hose, where only a trickle of water is coming through. As you straighten them out, at first, you may not see much difference. Having the courage to change every belief that does not serve you and then living accordingly will allow the attributes of Spirit, blocked by those beliefs, to start flowing through you, expressing in the world as wealth, health, beauty, joy, and an abundance of everything you may need or desire.

No One Is Ever to Be Blamed for Anything, Including You

But *you* have to take action. No one can do it for you. You can be shown the way–be informed, encouraged, helped along–but the bottom line is that ultimately it's your decision and your action that will make your vision manifest in the world. Until you take one hundred percent response-ability–meaning "ability to respond"–for everything that manifests, you can't live your full potential because what exists will always be someone else's fault. When you believe that something is the fault of your partner, your boss, your upbringing, the government, the weather, or something, you have given away your power to those people or situations.

As long as you blame someone or something, you are not in charge of your life. And that doesn't mean being in charge of the events or the circumstances that happen. No! It simply means you are responsible for the response you have to events or situations. With a conscious response from the place of knowing you are your soul, and therefore circumstances are there only to help you evolve to your next level, you are one step closer to the level of your Spirit.

You are the captain of your soul, so no one outside of you has any power over you, for your conscious awareness claims that. As you keep taking inspired action, your trust in divine guidance will grow, and you will know what happiness is, even when it seems there is no outside cause for it. Your connection to Spirit will be the only cause.

Claim Your Full Potential

Even if you don't fully realize it, there is only one place where you have complete control, and that is over your own perceptions and actions. You may think you control your life, but you only cope with events as best you can. It would be logical for you to concentrate your efforts on where you know you can make meaningful changes, and that is in your own life, through your internal perspective. That depends on you, and you alone.

When faced with a situation you can't control, your feelings are the result of your perception. Imagine the feelings of Joe, a native who has never had contact with the outside world, and the only means of locomotion he knows is walking. When you take him out on a train ride, you want to show him how wonderful it is to be moving so fast and getting to a destination in an hour instead of days of running. You take him up front with the driver, where he can have an unobstructed view of all the scenery, including the train tracks, as far as they go.

When he sees them coming together in the distance and sees how fast he's going, he panics, thinking his last hour has come. What just happened? He was seeing the tracks coming together. Having always lived in a jungle, he didn't know about perspective. So he believed what his eyes told him, thought the train would crash when it got to those narrowed tracks, and freaked out. His experience and your experience of exactly the same situation, at exactly the same moment, were totally different.

This is what we all do in any situation we're faced with. We look at what's in front of us, and depending on our culture, upbringing, and capability of changing our perception, the experience we have of a situation can be either good or bad. All we need to do is change our perception, which will change our experience. Feeling powerless is only a belief–and a false belief.

THE POWER WITHIN: RECLAIMING YOUR RESPONSIBILITY

However, just understanding your belief is false is not enough. You also have to claim that power before it can be delivered to you in the 3-D world. This is what the biblical statement "Ask, and ye shall receive" (John 16:24) means. When you, as that infinite all-powerful Spirit, declare that you now have the highest understanding, knowledge, and clarity to achieve your desire, and that it's going to be joyful and effortless, everything will fall into place with ease, integrity, and in accordance with your divine purpose. It will be delivered to you. Know it–with a capital K–then listen to your intuition as to what actions to take, and trust in guidance.

Taking back your power implies you've given it away, by believing other people or circumstances have power over you, by waiting for someone or something to change before you can. You do not change facts, events, or outcomes; what you change is your experience of them.

Trust in the Wisdom of Source

Trust that everything that comes your way is always an opportunity for something new and something better to emerge on the other side of the painful experience. The Universe is always working for the highest good of everyone; Source that created you loves you unconditionally and only presents situations that will make you grow spiritually, even if materially things don't look so good. Source is only concerned with your spiritual evolution through the quality of your response to the circumstances that arise in the material world.

We will go much deeper into that in chapter 6, "The Power of Surrender." For now, notice it's only the egocentric perception of a situation that causes your negative feelings and reactions. It's always a good idea to take some time, when faced with something you don't like, to consider other aspects which may not be immediately apparent. So to take the example of Joe seeing the train tracks coming together: If he had taken time to connect to the Great Spirit, the source of all good, he might have realized this was just an experience designed to help him grow him in some way.

When you experience any situation that is uncomfortable or painful, first sit in communion with God and ask for illumination. What is God's view of the circumstance? Only after feeling divine love and support do you start physically doing something because now your frequency has been raised. Now you have access to more expanded ideas and perceptions that are in that higher frequency, to which you did not have access in a previous state of overwhelm or resistance. Connecting to Spirit will also make you mindful of the responsibility not to add to the discord of the world through your angry, resentful, or frustrated thoughts and actions. Not that we can ever really add to the darkness of the world, because darkness is not a thing; it has no existence of its own. It's just the absence of light. So if we don't add light, we simply contribute to maintaining the level of darkness.

Whatever situation you find yourself in, start becoming aware that it's your feeling of disconnection from Source that is causing the judgments you have about the event being unfair or unacceptable, which contributes to your feelings of frustration, anger, overwhelm, or fear. Because if you did feel connected to Spirit that is all perfection, none of these thoughts or feelings could possibly appear. Therefore, first make your connection to Spirit by consciously switching your attention to the beauty, harmony, peace, and joy that is everywhere in nature, if you're willing to look.

The qualities of Spirit can only become apparent in 3-D through its expressions, of which you are one. If you allow it to pour through you, its goodness will always be showing up in and around you. As Derek Rydall, the well-known spiritual teacher, says, the word *man* in ancient Sanskrit means "the dispenser of divine gifts."[5] You are meant to transmit and express the divinity within you out into the world so it can come back to you. Written in the Bible, "Cast your bread upon the surface of the waters, for you will find it after many days . . . " (Ecclesiastes 11:1) simply means that as you give, so you shall receive. But in order to give anything, you must first have it.

The first step is to realize you have all the qualities of Spirit. The second step is to awaken those you desire from their dormant state into an active state. That is done through giving to yourself the love, the joy, the compassion, the peace, whatever it is you most desire to have. Love yourself as the God you are. Once you feel filled with that love, appreciation, and validation, you activate the law of circulation by offering it to every other expression of God. What does not circulate becomes stagnant and eventually dies.

You keep life circulating in your body by breathing. Notice that the first act in your life at birth is to breathe in, giving to yourself. Only afterwards do you breathe out, giving that life force to the Universe around you. The same law of circulation applies to every quality you desire: fill yourself up first from your Source, then start giving it out to others, or the energy stagnates and festers.

Life demands a balance, and the law of circulation ensures that balance. Where there is no inflow and outflow in a pond, it becomes stagnant, devoid of life, and ultimately dries up. This also applies when there is just a trickle of inflow but no outflow. You first receive from Spirit; you activate that, live it, and give it out to the world. Next you wait for it to be reflected back to you and receive it. Then you can give it out again, keeping the circulation going. Most of us are not yet very good at receiving because we have been giving and giving, sometimes to the point of becoming exhausted and burned out. You know what they tell you when they give the safety instructions in a plane? Put your own oxygen mask on first before assisting others. You can only help them if you are breathing and secure. It might be a good idea to look after your own needs first before helping other people, or you might not be there for them at all.

Any Change in the World Must Start with Changing You

All power is within, because, through the simple fact of having life, you possess all spiritual qualities. And by that same token, everyone else in the world also has everything they need. So if you have a perception that something is missing, the easiest way to obtain it must be to turn to Divinity and become aware of having that quality–or in the case of material desires, of having the quality that material thing represents.

The first step of allowing the power of your Spirit to flow–by straightening out the garden hose–is changing your limiting beliefs and understanding you are powerful. The next step is actually obtaining what you most desire in life, usually material things. Everything material, without exception, represents some spiritual quality, and they are all dormant in you. Divine qualities become material things when brought into the physical world through action.

Everything material is just a representation in physicality of some divine quality that is always spiritually present and fills a need. Everything has a purpose, even if we don't see or understand it. Take the page of the book you're reading: it represents flexibility; smoothness; symmetry of two long sides and two shorter ones; intelligence, when you look at the content of the writing on it; inventiveness, since someone had to figure out a way of putting ideas into solid form to make others in far-off lands benefit from them. Look at a flower: it represents beauty in its color; harmony in its form; the laws of mathematics in the number of petals, sepals, and stamens; fulfillment for the bees that come for its honey; pleasure in its scent.... Everything material usually represents many qualities. What is your desire right now? Determine the qualities that desire represents, and take the actions that will anchor that particular quality in you. Or stop behaviors that feel incongruent with your desire.

Any change you want to see in your life must start with changing you: your thoughts, feelings, and actions. Turning to someone or some situation in your life and asking them or it to change so you can feel more loved or respected or appreciated, must result in failure because they may not want to change; the way they are suits them best. And we have very little to no control at all over people or events outside of us.

If it's more money that you want, getting together at a coffee break and agreeing with the general conversation that the economy is bad, or the corporations keep all the profits for themselves, is not the best way of going about it. When you do that kind of thing, you have just stopped the manifestation of your prayers for more abundance, or negated affirmations that you have millions of dollars flowing to you.

When you start living your life from a place of loving, respecting, and appreciating yourself, and others see how things always seem to work out for you, how nothing seems to bother you, they will want to learn your secret. Then you can tell them, "I am endeavoring to live my life from the perspective of the Source that created me, loves me, and would never harm me in any way. Therefore, anything that seems difficult or painful just shows me where I am not congruent with Source. Life gives me an opportunity to see things in a different light, and when I do, everything seems to work out perfectly."

You can look at life as if it was a play, with you as the main character in the play that is your life, acting out what you have scripted for yourself, even if now you don't remember having done it. Everyone else is the main character in their own play, choosing their path for the outcome they scripted for themselves. Only you know what's best for you; everyone else knows what's best for them, and their experiences are exactly what they need to get to their destinations. Therefore, your opinion of what is best for someone else has no value whatsoever.

Incidentally, all destinations are the same, and that's realizing the wholeness and completeness of God. That's the meaning of the word *predestination*. The only uncertainty is the road you take to get there, and your free will determines that. It might be easy and pleasant, or difficult and winding around many obstacles. That is how you reconcile the paradox between there being a predestination, and also having free will.

You Can Choose the Perception You Wish to Have

Your free will allows you to choose the perception to have. The two main choices are the spiritual perception, that of Source, and the material perception, that of the personality. The spiritual perception is unity, oneness, wholeness, and perfection of every situation. The material perception, rooted in duality, can be the whole spectrum of perceptions less than the perfection of Source. Those can easily be changed, as when we get to see someone else's point of view.

We can place ourselves on top of a hill and see the surroundings from that higher perspective, or go to the bottom of the valley and see the same surroundings from a different angle. The actual surroundings are the same, but we see them very differently. When we spot a panther on a mountain road, that's a fact. If we think, *this is danger*, we feel afraid and start running. On the other hand, if we think, *he's beautiful*, we feel love, and stay put just to look at him longer. The event was the same, but our perception of it was different, which triggered a different feeling and a different response.

That's a true story: it happened to me some time ago. I was walking a trail in the woods, and suddenly a mountain lion appeared on the path, maybe thirty feet away–I didn't see or hear him come. He had little round ears, a long tail, and shiny, sleek fur. The only thought in my head was *He's so beautiful!* I couldn't tear my eyes away, until I just looked at an empty path. I didn't see or hear him go. He had moved with amazing speed.

My reaction was certainly due to my long years in Africa and many safaris. Mostly, the way we view events has been learned from our parents, teachers, or other people we meet and whose opinions we value. They may have been true or valid when we were children, but may no longer be valid now we're adults. Of itself, what appears has no meaning; it only takes on the meaning we give it. And it's our sacred responsibility to choose the meaning that will be the most beneficial, from the point of view that we are Spirit just having a physical experience. Choosing from a false perspective can only lead to a labyrinth of other choices, each one getting worse, until we reverse our thinking and start choosing from a true one.

Taking Back Your Power

In chapter 1, you discovered that there is only one Power, and that it's everywhere; so it's right where you are, and, therefore, you are that point of power. Now you are realizing you can't access that power until you move from being a victim to taking full personal responsibility; not responsibility for events or situations, but for your perceptions, thoughts, and actions regarding those events. In the victim mode, you have given away your power to people or circumstances; it's time to take it back, through consciously choosing your focus and your response.

But how do you start feeling empowered and strong in a situation that seems hopeless? This can be done through reconnecting with your true nature, which is Spirit, the "I" inside of you that is all-powerful, all-knowing, and all love. Spirit lives as you, just waiting to express the joy, harmony, intelligence, peace, and abundance it always is through you.

So look at some area in your life where you seem to be stuck, struggling, or unhappy, or where you don't know what to do. Observe the thoughts and the feelings you have about that situation, without judgment. Simply notice your feelings about it. *It's unfair. I don't deserve this. Who do they think they are? They don't understand. I've been patient, and this is the result* . . . . Whatever your thoughts and feelings are, just observe them and notice that they feel kind of heavy and hopeless, maybe even fearful or humiliating. It's a lower, denser vibration and frequency. Even the possible solutions for your issue have a heavy, helpless feeling about them. You don't really believe they will work.

That's because every problem has its own specific frequency where it lives. When your thinking and feeling matches that frequency, the problem manifests in your life. If you manage by sheer willpower, either by moving to another town or resigning from your job to solve your problem, it will only be temporary. A similar problem will again manifest in your new job or new location simply because you have not altered your frequency; you've taken it with you wherever you go. Think back to the analogy of ice being your problem and melting it with boiling water. Even if the problem gets better temporarily, soon it will come back worse than before because you have not addressed the root cause, the low temperature.

Exactly the same thing is true about the parts of your life where a problem appears. You simply cannot solve it if you remain at the level of thinking that brought it into your life. When it seems as though other people are the cause, that's never true; it's your vibration that brought it into your life. All you have to do is consciously shift your thoughts to a past happy situation, or anticipate a future happy event and stay in that feeling, even if it's for a minute at a time. Incrementally, your vibration will rise, and you will have longer periods when the painful or disturbing thoughts no longer paralyze you.

Your body does not know the difference between reality and imagination, nor the difference between past, present, and future. Its frequency responds to what you imagine exactly the same as if it were real now, whether you are thinking of a past event or anticipating an amazing future. The feelings you have now are the very substance of the future that will be manifesting; your tomorrow is made of what you are feeling today. Similarly, your today is made of the overall essence of your feelings of yesterday. So when you want to raise your vibration out of the frequency of your problem, let your thoughts dwell most of the time on happy situations. It doesn't matter if they're in the past or in a happy future. The result will always be a higher vibration.

There is always an alternative way of viewing anything that shows up in your life when you stand in your power as divine Spirit. All the attributes of Spirit are waiting for you to radiate and pour them out into the world at large, according to your particular talent. What if every lack or limitation you have is not something negative you have to clear, but an opportunity for you to recognize and let out the opposite quality you're already filled with as Spirit? What if the outside world was always presenting you with new opportunities to make higher choices than you have made in the past? If you see anger, whether towards you or between other people, start radiating peace. If you see greed operating, radiate cooperation. If you notice criticism or judgment, activate tolerance and compassion. When circumstances are such that you can't do it out loud, then just do it inwardly, and you will have added some light to the balance of light versus dark in the world. Darkness is just an absence of light. And as we've already seen, every time you add light, some of the darkness gets dissolved.

> What if we were all so busy adding light to the world that there was no time left for thinking about clearing out darkness? There would be nothing left but Light!

What if we were all so busy adding light to the world that there was no time left for thinking about clearing out darkness?

There would be nothing left but Light!

Review of chapter 2:
- ⟡ When in consciousness you are one with Spirit, you can change your life.
- ⟡ You are responsible for your life because it's happening *through you, not to you.*
- ⟡ Your focus, perceptions, and beliefs, which are the only things you can change, determine your experience.
- ⟡ It's the end of being a victim.

CHAPTER 3

THE POWER OF SELF-AWARENESS: CHANGES MUST BE DONE

Imagine you're in a huge three-story mall, and you're looking for the shoe store called Extravaganza Shoes. Wandering around the mall looking for what you want will take a long time. You don't know where the store is in relation to where you are, and soon you are completely lost—sure you've passed this way already and not knowing where to turn. A large poster catches your eye, with a huge arrow that says, "You Are Here!" It shows a plan of the three floors of the mall, with every store identified by name; and the arrow is pointing to a precise spot on the map. Wow! You now know where you are. You can look for the name of your store and find the shortest path to it. Certain of where to turn and where to go up or down, you'll get there fast, without getting lost. Going to buy shoes in the mall without knowing where you are in relation to the store is like your not knowing how to get what you want in life because you don't know where you are either mentally or emotionally.

Extend the analogy to wanting to get happiness, health, wealth, or success. You get lost in the stories of your life, looking for what you want in the things you can see in your job, your parents, friends, partner, and all the various outer structures. None of those seem to really fulfill you.

Not until you position yourself and see that you are a spiritual being having a human experience–and therefore having divine guidance as to what to do and where to turn–do you start to really move towards your goal with the certainty of reaching it in the shortest possible time. But you must move. It will not be done for you.

Get Honest and Real with Where You Are

If you want to move your life from where it is to where you want it to be, first know exactly where you are with total honesty–without the story, excuses, or embellishments as to why. First, see if you have been avoiding facing your issues by praying, meditating, and affirming the opposite, while hoping God would do something about it. Perhaps you've been blaming life, your boss, your partner, or your family for not supporting you, and for being the way they are. All of these are just tactics for not really acknowledging that the situation, whatever it is, has nothing to do with anyone else. Now is the time to consciously accept this and sit with it. Examine, piece by piece, where you want to make the changes that will be meaningful and will improve your experience.

My Getting Honest with Where I Was

As I was looking at the layout I did for this chapter, I got overwhelmed. I couldn't do this. There were too many directions in which to go, too many different ideas bumping against each other. I couldn't tie them together. I wasn't good enough. Why did I ever even consider that I could embark on such a task as to write a book? It's too big, too many ramifications. I'll never finish it. I don't know enough. I am not a teacher! Here I am only in chapter three, and I'm stuck. My writing is terrible; no one will want to read it anyway. I don't even know where to start! I don't know how to explain things! I am incapable, unequipped for this. No one ever listens to me. So maybe the idea of writing is just my way of trying to compensate for people not listening to what I have to say, not interested, even laughing . . . .

Suddenly, I realized those feelings that were getting worse by the minute could have nothing to do with the simple task of just writing a few pages. I was overreacting, getting lost in stories that had nothing to do with what I had set out to teach in this chapter, which is self-awareness. I was literally living, right now, the principle I wanted you to truly get today. Was I really aware of what was going on inside me? All this pressure, feeling unworthy, ridiculous, wanting to give up just because of writing a few pages–it didn't make sense. This was causing me to react in ways I really didn't like. I got angry with myself, and that didn't help either. I thought I was reacting to my writing. I believed I was incapable, less talented than others, that I lacked creativity and knowledge, but it's out of proportion. Is it even true? There must be something else here. So I started first identifying then exploring each feeling as it came up.

Have I ever had those feelings before? In what situations, what circumstances, and why and where did I feel them in the past? How often? Here is what my feelings of overwhelm and unworthiness brought up and how they surfaced.

Overwhelm: This feeling brought pictures of schools and too many children to deal with when I'd only ever been home-schooled with two cousins. The teachers paid no attention to me: I didn't belong, I wasn't accepted, I shrunk into my shell. Then another school in a foreign language: I felt (and certainly was!) inadequate, my work rated not good enough, my essays marked F. Another school in another language: more overwhelm, and everyone laughed at my efforts to communicate. All my negative feelings about myself were being reinforced. Behind in some subjects, ahead in others, my experiences and beliefs about life were unlike, if not totally opposed to, those held in this new world. I avoided sharing my ideas, or speaking at all. The negative feelings about myself far outweighed the positive aspects. And no one was teaching me to just focus on the good things in life while dealing with the not so good. More and more jumbled images kept coming–once you start, it's hard to stop them appearing!

Unworthy: This brought up an image from the war years. I was about eight, in a tram, and being laughed at and threatened with a dagger by two German boys bigger than me. I just knew it was because of my nationality, and they thought themselves superior. I was inferior, a nonentity. This triggered such anger, it blinded me to common sense; I grabbed the dagger and threw it down. He was so surprised that it worked, and I got off the tram in a hurry. I could relate that to the anger at myself now, when writing.

Other images from my childhood cropped up about decisions I had made and beliefs I had formed about myself. My grandfather looking down at me frowning, and what I wanted to say stuck in my throat. *He doesn't want to hear what I have to say.* My grandmother telling me never to tell anyone I had seen the Jew she was hiding from the Germans as we would all be in trouble, and he would be taken to a concentration camp. *Never speak about anything you know. It's trouble.* Getting a beautiful book all about dinosaurs for my birthday and hearing the comment, "She's much too young to understand all that." And that rankled. *I'm stupid.* All the kids in the class laughing at me when I stumbled over a word and the teacher saying, "That's enough of that, she doesn't know English," and I felt so ashamed, different, and incapable. My boss saying, "I have two secretaries, one's stupid, the other a foreigner!" *I'm different; I don't belong.*

All the decisions I had made then–not to speak, not to interact with people, to stay invisible, all the beliefs of not being capable, not good enough–I could see them now all playing out again and again in my life. And so many times when I started on a new idea, or was on the verge of achieving something, this feeling of it being

THE POWER OF SELF-AWARENESS: CHANGES MUST BE DONE

too much, of my being incapable, came over me. So I just gave up: it wouldn't work out anyway, so why try. Does this sound familiar? I now saw that what I was feeling was that pattern I created in my childhood; it's those old beliefs, and not what's in front of me right now. I'm not really here writing this chapter, but rather I'm in class trying to read through strange words, or not being listened to, or being ridiculed.

Patterns Run Our Lives

The meaning, the usefulness of a pattern, is so that you can become aware of it and examine it to see if it still serves in the light of who you are now, both as a human and a spiritual being. You will easily forget just one occurrence of failing; if you fail at something over and over it will incite you to look at why it's happening, and where you can make an adjustment. You can react as a five-year-old, with tears and a tantrum, or a spiritual being of love and understanding. This time, I recognized the patterns of rejection, frustration, and inadequacy. I could choose to continue to believe them, or see that they no longer applied to my life as it was now. I decided I will not retreat, nor give up, but instead will do my very best to show people they, too, can achieve the life they aspire to. When I came back to the writing, I could actually be present in this moment as the adult, rather than the inadequate little girl.

So what is really running *you*? What are the patterns in your life, whether private or professional? Where are you saying, "This always happens to me!" or "They always say that!" or "I never get to do what I want!"? Whether it's people being disrespectful, or you being disregarded, or people never keeping their promises, or you getting yourself into financial trouble, it's all a pattern that you need to break out of. It's probably a pattern established very early in life. Once you become aware of where and how it started, you can see how the pattern no longer applies to the adult you are. So it's up to you to no longer allow it to operate. We will be doing some of that work in the next chapter. But for now, just become fully aware of where your problems lie exactly.

What's really going on in your mental and emotional world when you find you're strongly reacting to a situation? You may be in a relationship that no longer feels good, in a job that seems to lack integrity, or in an environment where you are not appreciated. Just think about that for a moment; look objectively at the situation you're in now, or have been in recently. Is your reaction out of proportion to the facts? Just look deeper and see whether you're not actually in some past experience.

How the Mind Works

When you're feeling stuck, frustrated, unloved and not good enough, stop! Realize you are overreacting to a remark your partner made, to the criticism of your boss, or to a situation, and then become aware of the feelings you have. When did you feel them before? Probably many times, even back to your early childhood. So you are not really present to this situation, you are reliving past experiences stacked on top of one another, most of which you don't even remember. But often, you will remember the one that started it all, or at least one of the early memories.

We really have two minds, a conscious and a subconscious. Your conscious mind is focusing on the task you're doing, and the subconscious one is like a recording machine that has stored all the thoughts and experiences of the past, everything you have learned from the day you were born, so that you can pull it up whenever necessary without thinking about it. The subconscious mind is often blamed for your unthinking reactions. How often have you said, "I don't know why I said that, or did that!"? But it is also very useful. Once we have learned to walk or drive a car, both difficult in the beginning, we don't have to relearn them every morning.

THE POWER OF SELF-AWARENESS: CHANGES MUST BE DONE

Once recorded in the subconscious mind, they become automatic. We can keep walking while reading a book; we can keep our mind on the conversation with a friend while driving a car. Have you ever arrived at the office and realized "I don't even remember how I got here!"? So your subconscious mind is a friend, allowing you to do many things automatically, while the conscious mind can be focusing on other things.

How the Subconscious Mind Works

There could be no progress without the subconscious mind. It's just like a recording machine: it stores everything, both the music you want and the slamming door you would rather not hear again. A past traumatic experience that made us react with fear, or made us believe we are unloved, establishes a program in our minds to react a certain way every time a similar event happens. Every similar experience reinforces the belief that this is dangerous, or that we're not good enough, or unloved.

For example, when you were five years old and happy to be home after school, dancing around, jumping on the sofa, and wanting everyone to hear the funny song you just learned, you felt you had achieved something! Then your mother tells you to be quiet and stop making so much noise. All at once you feel totally deflated, unappreciated, unwanted, unloved. You feel reprimanded when you haven't done anything wrong; no one is interested in you or wants to know of your achievements. When reinforced by similar occurrences, it becomes a pattern of shutting down, not expressing yourself, feeling not deserving of love and unappreciated–when in reality, your mother just had a headache, or your father had work to do and needed peace.

That child's interpretation of an event at the age of five had nothing to do with the facts. The parents absolutely loved and appreciated her, but just needed calm in that moment. The pattern, however, had been started and will play out again and again, until she recognizes it with an adult's mind, traces it back to its origin, and examines whether it's still applicable now.

Steps to Determine Whether Your Feelings Are Just Patterns

So what's really going on when you overreact in the present without realizing you're not here and now? Taking the example of me writing this chapter, I will lay out for you the steps I went through to lift myself out of the negativity.

First, it was just feeling frustrated, overwhelmed, that this was too difficult, and wanting to give up.

Second, I realized I was overreacting to what was actually in front of me. These feelings had nothing to do with writing because I could actually write. Whether it would be appreciated, or make sense to anyone else, was quite another matter.

Third, I identified each feeling; gave it a name, a label; wrote them down; and searched my mind for when I had felt them before. Images came up: specific instances with my grandfather, at school, being a less-than, incapable, a foreigner.

I examined each one with an adult's mind, seeing them for what they were in actual fact. My grandfather may have been just focusing on what I had to say, not rejecting me. The kids in school were just having fun. My boss was projecting his frustration on the two obvious possible culprits. As a child I was not able to reason this way; the patterns of being a foreigner, incapable, and not listened to still played out even up to this moment. Before this, I wasn't aware and couldn't see them for what they really were.

Last, the awareness of past feelings allowed me to make the decision they will no longer interfere in my present life. No more! I now had a choice: to keep acting as a five or ten-year-old, or as an adult knowing my power as a divine being.

THE POWER OF SELF-AWARENESS: CHANGES MUST BE DONE

When I identified my feelings, traced them back, and really saw they no longer served me and were not even applicable to the person I was now, I became that arrow in the mall that said, "You Are Here." I knew my goal, the writing, knew where I stood as an adult and spiritual being, and realized that I could go straight to my destination without being sidetracked in the alleys of doubt and fear.

Programs Are Coping Mechanisms

The programs established throughout your life are coping mechanisms, designed to ensure your safety or very survival. As a race, our survival is now assured, with over 7.5 billion people on the planet. Even our safety, in most instances, is assured, unlike the days of living in a cave when wild beasts could have devoured you if you hadn't been constantly on the lookout for possible danger.

Now, your life is run largely on autopilot. Ninety-five percent of the time you are operating from established various programs, and, mostly, they serve you well. But the progress of humanity has taken a new turn on the spiral of evolution and many of our beliefs as to how life really works are being challenged by global events. The Newtonian model of life is found to be inaccurate by modern science, and many of our beliefs and behaviors must therefore also be changed.

Changing well-established habits and beliefs is difficult, uncomfortable, and often inconvenient, even when intellectually you want to change them because the subconscious programs clash with your new understandings, insights, and desires. You are consciously present to what you're doing only 5 percent of the time, and that is not enough to make the shift and achieve real progress. Consider the amount of time you have devoted from the age of five or so right up to college, progressively learning new things until you have internalized them, so most of them have become automatic.

You must reprogram your subconscious mind to abandon certain beliefs, to make it align with your new understanding of how life works and what you currently want. That's not easy, because your mind views the new idea or belief as a virus, an attack on what it thinks is safe. Any change spells death to the ego, and it will resist with all the arguments it can conjure such as: your new understanding will not get you the recognition of your peers that you value because they hold different views; and you will lose the love of your life because they don't believe what you now believe. It will take time, courage, and consistent effort on your part to keep your new understanding in the forefront of your mind, even when your eyes and ears tell you a different story. The Scriptural words "Judge not according to the appearance, but judge righteous judgment" (John 7:24) simply mean to look at spiritual Truth, not material appearances.

It's really beneficial to become fully conscious and examine your automatic responses, especially the ones that leave you sad, depressed, angry, or frustrated, to see whether or not they really serve you. Then change any automatic responses so that unconscious programs won't run your life.

Understand Your Story and the Patterns Running You

I heard this roar, a deafening sound I'd never heard before. It came from the sky. There was a plane close overhead, and it was going down. Something was wrong. Smoke was trailing behind it, and in seconds it had disappeared behind the trees. There was an earth-shaking explosion, flames and smoke shot up high into the sky.

I found myself under a bush, hands over my ears, screaming. I didn't know what was happening. Someone pulled me out, and we ran back to the house. I was four, and this was the beginning of World War II. But what happened in the days that followed was, for me, even worse.

THE POWER OF SELF-AWARENESS: CHANGES MUST BE DONE

I had lots of rabbits in a large, high chicken-wire enclosure with bushes, trees, and fallen logs where they liked to play. The kitchen would provide me with cabbage leaves, lettuce, and carrots, and the rabbits would come to eat from my hand. I often went to sit on a tree trunk inside to watch them running and chasing each other. When war started, my whole family left the country house where we lived for Cracow, a large town in the south of Poland. We went in horse-drawn farm carts, and I was devastated at having to leave my rabbits behind with no one to look after them. I pleaded and cried, but nothing helped; everyone was busy and had no time for me. I was alone, sad, abandoned, unloved, not allowed to go and sit with my rabbits; we were leaving without them.

There are some events that influence and impact our lives in a deep, unrelenting way. For me, those were some of them. I didn't realize how that plane crash had impacted me for over seventy-five years, until I came to grips with it. And so did abandoning my rabbits. What are the events in your life that have really impacted you? What are the rabbits in your life that have established your patterns, have triggered the deeper themes and ongoing experiences for you? Loss, abandonment, betrayal, insecurity, helplessness? What can you learn from them, so you can get the lesson and access the hidden strength and blessing?

Without Awareness We Don't Have Conscious Choice

It's important to become aware of whether your reaction is appropriate to the present situation, or you are run by programs, having given your power away to beliefs and perceptions without questioning if they are true.

Many of our beliefs have evolved since childhood, but some are still active such as that we are powerless human beings separate from God and His goodness and that we must attract and get from outside what we need or desire. As soon as you truly realize you are that all-powerful Spirit expressing through and as you, you can no longer pretend to be a victim of circumstances. You start to perceive events and situations from another perspective; you'll have different thoughts and feel more empowered. Maybe it's time to ask why you have not chosen to think differently before? It's simply because you were unconscious, unaware you had that choice. You were living your life just reacting to what was in front of you, which was a reaction learned from many past similar situations. When you have a reaction rather than a response, you are not actually reacting to the current situation in this moment, but to something, usually in your childhood, that had made you feel a similar emotion and from which you created a belief about yourself or about life. It has become a filter, a shadow through which you now habitually see, a belief that you are unsafe, unsupported, or unloved.

> What you carry in your consciousness you will observe outside.

We have all heard the saying that we believe what we experience and have actually seen it play out, as when people complain, "This is always happening to me." These individuals are holding an awareness of past, similar occurrences. Whatever you hold in your consciousness will surface again and again, since the outside world is just a mirror for your consciousness. This holds true for both negative and positive beliefs; but, unfortunately, what most sticks in your mind are the unpleasant things. What you carry in your consciousness you will observe outside. When you listen to news reports of robberies, houses broken into, and people attacked in the streets, notice how you start hearing about such things more often and then begin to see it happening to people you know. Next, your place gets burgled or your purse stolen. This didn't happen because there are suddenly thieves around;

THE POWER OF SELF-AWARENESS: CHANGES MUST BE DONE

there have always been thieves, and perhaps always will be. It happened to you because you were holding those beliefs in the forefront of your mind.

The beliefs we hold affect not only our outside experiences, but also everything that concerns our health. Bruce Lipton's book *The Biology of Belief* documents at length his research and findings on this subject. It's a fun book to read. It makes you understand how these things work and how to apply the knowledge in your life. He writes, "Your beliefs act like filters on a camera, changing how you see the world. And your biology adapts to those beliefs. When we truly recognize our beliefs are that powerful, we hold the key to freedom."[1]

Since you would never consciously wish for painful or distressing experiences, and yet they seem to be in your life, they must stem from subconscious beliefs. It makes total sense to examine the beliefs you hold unconsciously.

That is not to say that the subconscious mind is bad. In fact, it's extremely valuable. We've already seen that we live 95 percent of our lives from the subconscious mind, while only 5 percent from the conscious mind. That's when we are actually thinking of something specific like a project, solving a problem, or booking a flight. While we are doing that, it's our subconscious mind that takes over and lets us breathe, digest, walk, look right and left before crossing a street, drink a cup of coffee without spilling it, and drive while talking with a friend.

That subconscious mind is a repository of all experiences learned since birth. Up until the age of six or seven, we are like a sponge, indiscriminately absorbing everything that is going on around us. We just take in the beliefs of our parents, teachers, family, friends, and our own experiences. Primarily, we're in a kind of hypnotic state, where there is not a clear distinction between the real and the imaginary. Look at a boy who's riding a broom like a horse. You might want to sweep up, and ask him to give you the broom. He won't understand what you want; he's riding a horse. There is no broom.

So you have downloaded a whole lot of beliefs and information in the first seven years of life that you are now operating from, at the subconscious level. They're not yours, for they come from people "in authority" and may not even be true. Those beliefs become patterns that run automatically when a similar emotion gets triggered by any event or situation. For example, when you didn't get that amazing Halloween costume you wanted, you might have felt so disappointed, unloved, maybe even punished, even though you didn't do anything wrong. Now a situation arises where you don't get what you want from your spouse and your feelings of disappointment, of life being unfair, and being punished, are those of the five-year-old just replaying that old pattern. Until you bring those events or situations into your conscious awareness, examine them in the light of who you are now, and choose an appropriate response, there will be nothing you can do about the life those beliefs or feelings create for you.

So let's examine those patterns clearly and see what's really running you. By understanding the originating experience, you can see how it's connected and why it now triggers you. Notice how it has continued throughout your life. Uncover the bigger arc of this pattern, the deeper part of your story, because potentially there is a deeper life theme to discover that you need to recognize before you can be free from it.

The Seven Main Structures of Life

Look at specific situations in each of your life structures. Those are your relationships, work, health, wealth, personal development, service, and spirituality. You may have many challenges at this time; but for now, just pick one, the most important one, where you most want a change.

THE POWER OF SELF-AWARENESS: CHANGES MUST BE DONE

For example, in the area of relationships: Think about when your boyfriend or girlfriend didn't turn up, or turned up half-an-hour late. What were your feelings during that time? *They don't consider me, I'm not important, just a stop-gap, everything else takes priority* . . . . Consider where those feelings came from, when the truth of the situation was that your partner got stuck in a traffic jam, or their boss gave them a last-minute job, making them late. Maybe their phone battery ran out. Did you take the time to consider reasons other than your being unimportant?

What if your partner seems unsupportive and uninterested in what you want to do with your life? Perhaps it relates to money– you want to take that course on self-help, but in their view it's too expensive. Or they're so engrossed in their work that they never take time for a holiday, a weekend on the beach, or even a romantic dinner. Begin to really look at all the aspects of your relationships and honestly acknowledge how they make you feel. Are you feeling unloved, taken for granted, invisible? When did you first feel unloved, unimportant, invisible, or rejected? How often do you have those feelings about many other situations in your life?

In the area of work: Remember when you applied for that more responsible job, or a raise, and they didn't give it to you? You felt disappointed, devalued, and also angry, perhaps sad or depressed. Life is unfair! If that is a habitual reaction when you don't get what you want, or what you think you deserve, look at your early life when you got passed over so your younger sibling could play with the toy, or the time when you got punished for taking some cookies, but your baby sister didn't. Notice how the emotion or belief you have now started there. Those feelings have been reinforced by other events throughout your life. What are you really reacting to in this situation? Is it necessary to have those feelings, those reactions? Do they reflect the truth of the present situation? Do they serve you?

In the area of health: Have you ever faced a health challenge or received a diagnosis and immediately felt fear or despair because your mother and grandfather died from it, or your sister now has it with six months to live? So it runs in the family, and you think there's nothing you can do. You shrivel and contract, with feelings of anxiety or worry, not realizing that it's exactly those feelings that will stop your body from activating a healing response it automatically has when your feelings are peaceful and harmonious. Your body is wired to heal itself–if you will let it!

When you get a cut on your finger, do you get anxious and worry, or do you just put a Band-Aid on and forget about it because you know it will heal itself? You know worry never helps and actually makes your experience worse. Keeping your thoughts in the vibration of positive possibilities and happy outcomes–forgetting all about your diagnosis except when you are actually doing something to make yourself better–will help you get better mentally, emotionally, and also physically.

While we have explored the most prevalent life structures, take the time to look at the others as they might apply to you. What areas do you observe that might be lacking or insufficient, and how would you like to change them?

For many years, any sudden noise made me jump, reminding me of some traumatic experience in my past: the sound of running boots, the screech of brakes, the crack of a whip, sounds like gunshots. A fifteen-minute firework display used to leave me quite exhausted with tight and painful shoulders. I knew the explosions were coming and knew it was just fireworks, yet still I reacted until I consciously traced it back to that plane crashing and exploding when I was four years old. Your experiences of long ago don't have to continue impacting your life once you turn the light of your present understanding on them and become grateful, even if only for the insights you are getting.

THE POWER OF SELF-AWARENESS: CHANGES MUST BE DONE

Watch Your Own Reactions to Events

What were the traumatic events in your life? Perhaps you witnessed a swimmer who was dragged out to the ocean by the undertow of a crashing wave and just barely rescued–so now you are afraid to go swimming, even in a swimming pool? Perhaps you were six years old and wanted to go to the fun fair, but your dad or mum said, "No, we can't go," and you were so mad! And now, you find you're angry with your spouse for saying "no" to whatever it was you wanted–whom are you reacting to? Your mum or dad from thirty years ago, or your spouse now?

> You can't heal what you're not willing to feel.

Overreacting is a sign you're in an old pattern. That early event has become the filter through which you see your present experience. Examine every challenging situation to clearly see why and how you're doing things. Notice what your feelings and thoughts about it are. Look at your past to discover situations emotionally similar to the current one. See how the feelings and the beliefs you now have may have started there.

Now that you are aware, you are faced with a choice: whether to apply what you have discovered to your life, or continue living as before. And since you are still reading, I assume there are things that you want to change, that you do want to move forward and live a better and happier life.

I know becoming aware is difficult and can be uncomfortable, or even scary, because it's been really scary for me at times. I know you don't really want to go there; you just want to skirt over it. But really, you need to go there and feel it. You can't heal what you're not willing to feel. I've been there, and I know. I've been afraid of feeling my stories. I have tried to avoid going deep into the feelings of some situations that I've uncovered. I was afraid of reexperiencing the horrors and tragedies, and unwilling to endure the guilt, shame, grief, and rejection. I told myself how I didn't need to go there–it's over and finished. I learned to skirt the surface and thought I had it all together, had my life back again.

Yet it's never finished until you've totally faced and felt it, until you've looked at it in the present moment as the adult you are, the person you've become not in spite of it, but because of it. Only when I was willing to really go into all of it and unpack all the unresolved pain and resentment, hate and shame, did I also find the gifts and the power that lay hidden within every challenge. And to be quite honest, even now I still struggle with some of it. But every time I'm willing to be present with my story from the new place I stand in, I receive a new gift, and the story loses some of its power.

Deeper Meaning of Challenges

The deeper meaning of any challenge is that your soul wants you to evolve, to become a little more like itself. That's what you do through seemingly adverse situations. In a happy, joyful, harmonious situation, you are already one with Spirit, feeling the goodness and perfection. But as soon as you judge something as not so good, you have separated yourself from Spirit's perception, where nothing can be bad. Choose to place yourself as that "I" within you and see the event from its perspective, then you can have a higher response than the one you might have had on previous occasions. Even if it's just recognizing that, "This is an opportunity for me to grow in some way; I don't know how, but since it's here, it must be; help me see as divinity sees," instead of saying, "Why is this happening to me? It's unfair!" You move from being a victim to being a creator by choosing your responses.

Patterns that continue to run are really there to help you see the deeper theme of your life and why you have come into this world. If you are that omnipotent Spirit–and at some level, you know you are–in what way can you demonstrate it? You are here to learn how

THE POWER OF SELF-AWARENESS: CHANGES MUST BE DONE

to use the free will you've been given to align with the source of your being, rather than to separate yourself from it, and to see how to evolve to the next level, where those patterns and false beliefs will no longer sabotage the life you really want to live.

Based on what you now know, based on how your life has been unfolding, on the story you've been living and the patterns you've created, what changes can you make to improve your circumstances? You must be in that mall in front of the big arrow that says, "You are here!" because you know what you want and where you are. That lifts you out of being a victim and a problem-solver into being a creator and a vision-holder. You've given yourself permission to really feel what it's like to want what you want and to have what you want. You also know challenges are not there to stop you from advancing, but to make you evolve and grow spiritually and to make you stronger and more rooted in your invisible identity when the appearances of the material world show you a different picture. So all those wounds inflicted on your ego can be healed.

And in the next section, we will be doing just that.

Deal with Your Feelings

Now that you're fully aware, you can start the transformation process of healing all these feelings, correcting the false beliefs, and stopping the judgments you have about yourself and about life.

If I still remember having to abandon my rabbits, it's because the experience was a core wound of loss, abandonment, and separation that I had to heal. I felt they would die without me to look after them; I was their only friend. That was not really true, but genuine in my four-year-old mind. I felt I was not living up to my responsibilities, that no one listened to me or understood how vital it was I stay with them or they come with us, and that no one had considered what I wanted. So I felt unimportant, unloved, unsupported, irresponsible, and a coward: I had abandoned my friends! Loss and separation from everything and everyone I loved continued until I had nothing more to lose; only then could the reconstruction start on a different, higher basis. It was the shadows created in my early years that allowed me to develop the qualities that really serve me now. They stopped sabotaging me when I fully accepted and integrated those aspects I had been pushing away and trying to hide.

Working with your shadows will allow you to see their value. Integrate those angry and resentful parts of you and consciously make them your allies, rather than enemies that sabotage your goals. My mentor Derek Rydall has developed many ways for making friends with your shadows, two of which I will be giving you. But before working with the shadows you know about, I would invite you to look at some situations where you don't know what's happening–why you suddenly stop being motivated to complete some project, or you're afraid to move in the direction you previously felt was just the right thing for you. You want something on the one hand, but you're also afraid, so don't want it. When this happens, it may be that you have a values conflict, which is that you value certain things that seem to be in contradiction with some other things that you also value. This cannot be the truth because all goodness harmoniously coexists in Spirit, always; there is no quality that is in opposition to another one. It's only in your mind that the contradiction exists.

EXERCISE

I've adapted this exercise from Derek Rydall's teachings. For example, you value having money, and you also value spending time with your family. In your mind, money means hard work, long hours, and maybe even working on weekends, so enjoying time with family is not possible. You have created a belief you can have one or the other,

THE POWER OF SELF-AWARENESS: CHANGES MUST BE DONE

but not both. You are afraid of going for what you want, afraid of starting your business, afraid of investing in a program, afraid of failing.

The first thing to do is become clear on what are the things you value most in each of the life structures. And these are, as we've seen before, your health, finances, relationships, work, service, spirituality, and personal development. Make a list of all the things and qualities you value.

Take a piece of paper, right now, and write them down, so you have something in front of you to work with. Perhaps you value health, strength, flexibility, beauty, being vital and slim. You might also value having money, success, exotic holidays, your family, an amazing partner, and friends. You value being respected, validated, influential, and appreciated. Other things you value could be freedom, safety and security, prosperity, authenticity, being connected to Spirit, time for yourself, doing your artwork or music, engaging in an animal rights movement, or just hanging out with friends. Whatever it is for you, make a list of at least ten things and prioritize them, from the most important to the least important one.

Then take each one in turn, and ask yourself those four basic questions:

If you really had xyz:
- ❖ What would you lose?
- ❖ What won't you have?
- ❖ What will you have to sacrifice?
- ❖ What's the downside?

For example, if money is your priority: If I become really rich, I'll lose . . . what?
- ❖ Quality time with my family,
- ❖ Freedom,
- ❖ Privacy,
- ❖ Outings with friends,
- ❖ My alone time,
- ❖ I won't have real friends,
- ❖ People will want things from me,
- ❖ People will become jealous,
- ❖ I won't have time for my spiritual practice.

If spirituality is your priority: I'll have to sacrifice . . . what?
- ❖ The love of my partner,
- ❖ Going out with my friends,
- ❖ Having a well-paid job.

I'll lose . . . what?
- ❖ Respect or validation from others,
- ❖ Material success,
- ❖ Time for mountain climbing.

Whatever you came up with, it's not the Truth; however, in your mind, because of your life experiences and how things have played out in your family or environment, it seems to be the truth. You recall how your father had no time for you when he started his own business, and the toys you got did not compensate for your sadness. Or you saw how upset your best friend became when her parents divorced because her mother's time was totally taken up by her musical career. There is some belief in your mind that says, "I can't have a career and a happy family life," or "I can't be wealthy and loved," or "I can't be successful and healthy."

THE POWER OF SELF-AWARENESS: CHANGES MUST BE DONE

In my personal life, when I lived as a child under occupation and war conditions, I saw how dangerous it was to speak your truth, to say what you knew and believed in, or to be visible in any way. University professors, teachers, and priests were being imprisoned and tortured for teaching historical or religious truth; people were being killed and sent to concentration camps for their beliefs, or for just who they were. Any authority, in my mind, got a bad name because of the abuse of it.

So my search for spirituality could not be reconciled with being respected, supported, understood, and out in the open. When I started my work of healing others, I had less time for deep connection to God and meditation. That was another values conflict: I valued being of service in the world, and I valued my privacy and time for spiritual practice and deeper learning. Not until I started to weave those seemingly contradictory values together did I get to the next level of both my healing practice and honoring my spiritual needs.

My affirmation, a kind of a mantra, went like this: *"The more successful and active I am in the world, the more time, space, privacy, and connection to God I have; and the more I honor my need for time, space, privacy, and connection to God, the more successful and active I become in the world."*

It was adjusted from time to time, as my priorities and needs changed, but you can construct your own affirmation, taking your own values conflicts and making sure that you address them from both sides. So for example: *"The more wealth I achieve, the more I am loved and respected in the world. And the more respect, love, and validation I give to myself, the more productive I am in creating success and wealth in my life."* Write out your affirmation and keep it by your bedside, taped to your computer, or wherever you will often be reminded of it. And say it, multiple times a day, meaning every word of it.

That's a powerful way to work with your anxiety, procrastination, self-sabotage, and fear. In addition, while looking for possible values conflicts, you may have uncovered many shadows such as *I'm lazy, selfish, a failure, judgmental, helpless.* To encourage you to uncover a few more, and to work with them so as to embrace and integrate them, I would like to walk you through another process.

Finding Your Shadows

What we're going to do right now is look at an area where you're stuck, that's unpleasant and difficult for you, and where you feel something or someone needs to change before you can move forward. Maybe you're waiting for your own feelings or perceptions to change. This is Derek Rydall's basic idea, adapted by me.

Where do you want things to be different? You think that those Pilates sessions would do you a world of good, but after work you're too tired, your family is waiting for you, so you never get around to booking a session. You're not inspired to write that article or your book–you have no ideas. You want to prepare that amazing dish, but you never get to shop for the exotic ingredients.

Whatever it is for you, just look at where you are waiting for something or someone to change before you can move forward: either your boss, your partner, or your spouse needs to be different; your children take up less of your time; the economy, your finances, your health, or whatever else, needs to improve. Just think of one situation, right now, that you really wish would change.

What are your feelings about this situation? Are you disheartened or angry that you still don't have what you need? Maybe you're feeling that nothing ever works out for you, that life is against you. What are your feelings about yourself? You're a failure, a procrastinator, powerless, selfish, not good enough, incapable, frustrated, a bitch, or a jerk? All those are shadows you have created that are just crying out for your attention, recognition, and acceptance.

And so, what do you make it mean about yourself that nothing ever works for you? What kind of person would a boss, or their partner, treat that way? Someone who is worthless, incapable,

THE POWER OF SELF-AWARENESS: CHANGES MUST BE DONE

unlovable, fearful, indecisive, a doormat maybe? You're looking for some judgment about yourself that makes you feel bad.

When you have found the label, that quality you don't like, write it down. You may have found several. Write them all down; you can redo the process for each of them in turn. Then imagine yourself as truly successful in your field: how do you think people will judge you then? Superior, controlling, bossy–who do you think you are?! Those are also your shadows, so write them down.

Now that you have quite a few shadows, pick the one that has the most charge for you, the one that really makes you cringe when you imagine being called that. We only work with one shadow at a time, but eventually, you will be addressing them all, as you notice they need to be loved, accepted, and integrated. Because you are not getting rid of them, they each have gifts you can only access when you integrate those unresolved and unloved parts of you.

SHADOW EXERCISE

Now imagine there is an elevator in your head that takes you ten floors down from the mind into your heart. As the doors open, a most beautiful sanctuary is revealed. It can be a majestic temple, or your favorite spot in nature like a forest, a beach by the ocean, or a garden with tall trees and a profusion of colorful flowers. You hear birds chirping and see animals coming up to you with love in their eyes. Picture yourself in your sanctuary; perhaps you see a white marble seat with comfortable cushions, or just a tree stump, and you walk over to it, feeling the soft ground under your feet. The temperature is perfect. The delicate scent of the flowers and song of the birds adds to the peacefulness and beauty of the surroundings.

When you're ready, invite that quality or that shadow character–the angry, unworthy, or incapable part–to come for a talk. You will ask them some questions, and they will tell you what they're feeling and wanting. So call them in– just one at a time–and notice where they're coming from and what they look like: how they're dressed, how they move as they come closer. Ask them to sit in the seat next to yours, and start by asking them:

1. **What was the event that occurred in my life early on that caused me to reject you, or to create you? What was that event?** And you listen, or you can imagine a screen on which images, symbols, or glimpses of situations appear; maybe you hear words, or sounds. You may get images in your mind's eye, or just a knowing, a glimpse of a situation, or a sensation of an event that is hard to define, a vague feeling. Stay focused inside. Just listen and look. Don't think or judge anything that comes. **What was that event that caused me to reject you, or create you?** Allow yourself to receive all that you're noticing. Whatever emerges in your mind is perfect. Let yourself see, hear, or know. And then you ask:

2. **How have you been a blessing to me all along?** So far, you have been rejecting that part: trying to make it into its opposite, trying to make it a good boy or a good girl and not succeeding, and then trying to get rid of it by locking it up in the basement so it won't be seen or heard. But now you have changed. You understand they are a part of you and, as such, they deserve to be loved and accepted exactly like all the other "nice" parts of you. You have invited this shadow in to have a conversation, and you're realizing it has been your friend, helping you in spite of your bad behavior. So you say to them, "I am so sorry! Please forgive me; I will never reject you again, never try to get

THE POWER OF SELF-AWARENESS: CHANGES MUST BE DONE

rid of you, disregard you." Perhaps also ask them: **How have you been my ally; where have you assisted me in becoming better?** Let's say your shadow is "selfish," and you hear *I have taught you to be giving, to be generous, to become really selfless, and kind to others*. If your shadow is "incapable," it has motivated you to learn some skills, to get diplomas and degrees, which many people don't have. Your stupid self has pushed you into becoming really knowledgeable and skilled in your chosen branch. Find the blessing in your particular shadow–it's often the opposite quality. Your next question is:

3. **Why are you appearing to me now, what is your lesson or your gift to me now?** What are you here to tell me or to share with me now? What is it that's important for me to see now? Is there a different direction I need to take at this time? And listen to any insights, new ideas, different perceptions that may come up. Next you ask:

4. **What do you need from me to feel loved, supported, valued, validated, and safe, so that you can take a healthy place in my life?** Notice that you are not asking your incapable self to change. You are not asking the angry self to become peaceful or the sad self to become happy, and you're not asking the loser to become a winner. You are asking what *it* needs to feel accepted and loved and validated, appreciated and honored as an integral part of you. You have discovered it has been a friend and an ally even while you were disrespecting it; what kind of person would do that? Only one that has unconditional love for you, that totally supports you. So now, it's your turn to give your shadow whatever it needs–and it must come from you. So ask again: **What do you need from me, to feel loved, respected, and validated?** And listen for the answer that comes up from inside of you. Really listen. Not just for thirty seconds and say,

"Nothing is coming up!" Stay with it. Listen patiently. Say you love it, and you will never abandon it or push it away again; you will come back and listen to what it has to say every day, consistently, until it tells you what it needs. You will honor and love it because it's a part of you, even if it doesn't want to talk to you right now.

> Look back at any past situation, however difficult it was at the time, and you will always find a gift in there, and see some good has come out of it.

Imagine you had a child that you've been mistreating for years, and in the end saw how badly you behaved and wanted to make amends. So you sit beside the child and say, "I'm sorry for how I've treated you. I want to make it up; let's talk." How do you think the child is going to react? Do you think they're going to trust you straight away? It will take time for the child to respond to you, and they will need consistent proof of your good faith.

So if your needy or powerless self doesn't answer right away, keep asking, keep loving, and you will get an insight. You will get something like be more loving, or stand in your power, or speak your truth. That's a step in the right direction, but it's not enough for you to know exactly what to do. So keep asking, "Where am I supposed to be more loving? To whom do I speak my truth? How, when, where, to stand in my power? Ask until you get some specific answers, something you can actually do.

Whatever guidance you get, just make sure that you actually do what they requested; that's going to build trust that you really do want to get to know them, have them integrate into your life in a healthy way; not sabotaging you, but giving you the power that

THE POWER OF SELF-AWARENESS: CHANGES MUST BE DONE

so far you never had, because you were not whole. You had not accepted that energy as part of yourself.

By now you probably have one piece of guidance that you can act on. So I want you to embrace this part of you like you would a little child, hold it close and softly ask if there is anything else they want to tell you. And as you hold them listening to their whisper, they get smaller and smaller until they fit into the palm of your hand. Then place your hand over your heart and feel them integrating fully while you take a deep breath, feeling them becoming a part of you. Take another deep breath and just stay in that expansive place of integrating the first of those separate parts of you.

Looking for the gift in a current challenging situation is always difficult. We are too caught up in it and unable to see beyond it. But you can look back at any past situation, however difficult it was at the time, and you will always find a gift in there, and see some good has come out of it. In hindsight, you might even find it was the best thing that could have happened, because it has changed and evolved you in ways you would not have thought possible. The important thing now is to know that in the past, things have worked out in unsuspected ways, and project that into your future. Since you know that God is all there is, and is perfection, every situation must be for your ultimate good. Trust, and it will bring some peace of mind into any situation.

Finally, I invite you once again to bring into your awareness that challenge, that situation where you have found the shadow you have just worked with, the one that had the biggest charge. When you turned your back on it, it still gave you its gift. Now you've recognized it has never been your enemy; you've accepted it as having the same right to exist as any other part and asked for its forgiveness. And even if you haven't had time yet to do what it said it needed from you, your commitment for right now is enough.

Your shadow has begun to trust you. You will not disappoint it, and it will no longer sabotage your life.

Having done this deep work, perhaps you now feel a little more peaceful, confident, or empowered. Can you see some new possibilities or a different outcome from the one you feared? After doing the work on just one shadow, how does the situation feel now? What insights or new understandings have come up? What core growth or blessings can you see? And what will be possible in this area, when you love and embrace the shadows that you haven't yet had a conversation with? Take a few moments to visualize the life that can now unfold for you, a more empowered one, joyful, abundant, and harmonious. You are now able to fully claim the strengths made available to you through accepting and integrating those disowned parts.

You are now reclaiming your wholeness.

Review of chapter 3:
- ❖ You must get very honest with where you stand, mentally and emotionally.
- ❖ Your beliefs and conditions of early childhood have been the filters keeping you powerless. Recognizing they are only false beliefs that created your shadows gives you back your power.
- ❖ You cannot heal what you don't feel, so you allow yourself to feel all the unresolved pain and to heal your shadows.

CHAPTER 4

THE POWER OF PROBLEMS: USING CHALLENGES TO MAKE YOU STRONGER

One day, I woke up with a pain in my right foot. I never knew bones could hurt, but a bone right in the middle was painful. And kept getting more painful. Within a few days the foot had doubled in size, bright red verging on violet, the swelling creeping up to above my ankle. I could no longer walk, antibiotics made no difference, and words of "operation" and "gangrene" were bandied about. But somewhere, I knew there was no "reasonable" reason for it. I hadn't done anything to it.

Within a couple of weeks I couldn't stand, couldn't wear even a flip-flop. The pain was excruciating, and my leg had doubled in size. Apart from an operation, the only avenue left was turning to God. So I started asking, where am I making wrong choices? What could I do to heal this? What's the divine will for my life?

Days went by in constant questioning, but my condition was getting worse, until one evening, the image of two shamans and what they had said two and three years ago dropped into my head. I had never met either of them before. I was a healer, said the first one, and it was my choice to keep resisting it. It seemed so ridiculous I just laughed. A year or so later, another one told me the same thing and my reaction was exactly the same. I never even remembered I had been told that before.

Now, unable to walk and asking God for illumination, the shamans both dropped into my awareness, together with the absolute knowing that I had been shown my path twice over, at different times, and refused to go on it. The knowing that this was the reason for my problem, and this was what I was called to do regardless of my ability or capability, was so strong that it could not be ignored or denied. I just knew the problem would not be resolved unless I listened. Instantly, what shot through my mind was: "If You want me to do this, I will. But You have to bring me everything I need, because I don't even know where to start." It was a total absolute commitment such as I had never done before. With that, came a sense of peace, of "all is well" in spite of the pain and the added disquiet of having committed to something I had no idea how to accomplish. I went to bed more peaceful than in quite a while.

In the morning, the pain was almost gone, the swelling was halfway down and the next day the leg looked, and felt, as if it had never had the slightest problem. And in the next week, the first step of what I had to do was brought to me on a platter—and this time, I accepted and acted on it.

Problems Show We're Out of Alignment

Problems in general, whether physical, mental, or emotional, are just an indication of something we should do, or should no longer do. They make us conscious of our patterns. And mental or emotional problems, when not acknowledged, felt, and processed at the time they arise, are stored in the body and turn into physical problems. What do they symbolize? What are they really showing us? Issues with feet or legs symbolize not advancing in life, and right leg problems are connected with our own choices rather than random events.

I was seventy-five years old at the time, and thought I was already on a spiritual path, praying, reading, and meditating, with healing not even in my consciousness. So I got a message, twice over, in so many words, but did not absorb or act on it. The resulting pain in my body indicated that I had not listened to guidance. When I consciously started asking, "Show me what you want me to see, teach me what you want me to know, tell me what you want me to do," my body revealed where I had not listened to guidance.

The light bulb that went off in my head made me realize all these things in a split second. Instantly, I committed to honoring the guidance and doing the work required to become a healer.

So far, my spiritual path had been only a search for a deeper personal connection with God, and being of service in a spiritual community in very temporal ways. I thought that was my life-path and was happy doing it. Being a healer to others never entered my mind. I had heard of healing modalities, but had never been to see a healer, so being told I was one was just plain ridiculous – and certainly not true on a material level. So I dismissed the whole idea. But God's agenda for my life was not to just serve in a kitchen, and since I was not considering the ideas given to me through world-renowned spiritual leaders, other ways had to be found–and painful ones usually work.

In that split second when I saw the whole setup and committed to live God's agenda, a huge fear set in: I didn't know how! I had committed, had said "yes," and there was no going back on my word. But I had no clue as to how to even begin! The next thing was surrender: "I will do it, but You have to bring me all I need."

Then, before I had taken any concrete action, my own healing was done, even if it physically took thirty-six hours or so. Irrevocable commitment was enough; I saw how my problem was just a symbol telling me where I was out of alignment and where my life did not match my soul's agenda. I was given the clarity of what I had to do, and just the *commitment* to do it melted away the problem.

Notice I had started by asking God to resolve my issue. Instead of seeking a medical solution, I asked to be shown the reason for the pain and what I had to do to resolve it. When I realized

> Every external problem has an internal vibrational source, which is the way we think, the way we see life, what we believe about others and ourselves.

what was required–however scary and impossible it seemed–I committed to it. The healing of my discomfort had become secondary; my focus centered only on fulfilling my purpose. Not one fleeting thought went to whether or not it would help with my issue. My condition had not improved at all, yet I went to bed in total peace and contentment because I knew that my soul had traced a path that was irrevocable. The fact I woke up next morning almost without pain was a surprise, which simply reinforced my knowing that the problem was intimately connected to my resistance to a larger life that needed to unfold.

Vertical, Closer-to-Source Expansion Is the Divine Agenda

Many times our problems symbolize that more of our true Self is trying to emerge, but for some reason we're holding back. There is a bigger life trying to surface but we are resisting, often unconsciously. Somewhere, at some time, we have desired more for ourselves, particularly when starting out on a spiritual path to connect with the Source of our being. But we are not completely honoring it, we're not living in congruence with it, we're not letting it flow, so the energy gets stuck in the body, causing a problem. Every external problem has an internal vibrational source, which is the way we think, the way we see life, what we believe about others and ourselves. A problem cannot permanently be resolved without changing the vibrational source of it.

THE POWER OF PROBLEMS: USING CHALLENGES TO MAKE YOU STRONGER

Look at all the situations and events you uncovered in the last chapter, in any one of the structures of your life, whether it was your health, relationships, or work. Look at all the feelings of not good enough, selfish, unworthy, incapable, or whatever they were. See how they have helped you become more knowledgeable, more understanding, more compassionate. Go back over them: that problem in your relationship, or with your health, or that issue at work. What message is it giving you? What's the symbolic meaning? If you find any new shadows, go back to the shadow exercise we did in the last chapter and make sure you honor them for the gifts they have given you already, and reintegrate them into your life.

For me, looking at the real message behind the apparent problem, I realized I was not doing what my guidance had told me many times, in different ways. When I committed to it–shifted my thoughts 180°–the problem started dissolving almost instantly. It was just a symbol of a deeper, vibrational issue. When that was addressed, the lesson hidden in the problem was learned so there was no reason for the problem to continue.

Problems have a certain vibration, and if your vibration matches that of the problem, then you experience it, whether it's a lack of finances, an illness, or a relationship falling apart. They all live at their specific frequencies, just as the problem of ice lives at a frequency, or temperature, of 32°F. You can try to solve the problem of ice by chipping it away, pouring boiling water over it, or if you're really creative, using a flamethrower. But the problem will come back, because you cannot solve it while it's cold outside. The same holds true for your problems: they cannot be solved at the frequency where they live and where you are since you are experiencing the problem. If you raise your vibration closer to the vibration of Source, the problem will start to dissolve and disappear, just as the ice does.

As you evolve, rise to a higher level, a higher frequency, your problem cannot exist at that level. It appears that the problem gets solved, or disappears in some way. But what's really happening is that it cannot exist at the new, higher level that is closer to Spirit. It still exists for people who function at a lower frequency; they may still have the disease, be in debt, or be unhappy with their spouse. Not you, not any longer! Because inherent in every problem is the message, the guidance, and the mechanics for your evolution in that particular area, and you have grasped that message.

Core Wounds Are Initiations

Remember, you created those experiences and challenges as the quickest way to grow and express more soul-qualities. Your core wounds are really core initiations that set you on a journey of healing and forgiveness that affects the whole planet through the principle of oneness. Problems are just mechanisms to uncover your greater potential. They are catalysts for your growth and evolution. If your life was totally happy, every one of your desires immediately fulfilled, would you ever look for other avenues, bigger possibilities, doing other things? Probably not, and in the long run, this would lead to stagnation and regression because it is not possible to stand still. You either advance, grow, become more, or you regress, get smaller, and become less. When things are not so good, or when what you call problems show up, these are catalysts for new growth, new evolution.

Just as a forest fire seems quite a problem, and it is, at a certain level. It destroys the forest and burns everything up. But certain trees, like the jack pine, actually need the intense heat of the fire to melt the glue sealing the cones to release the seeds that hold the potential of new growth to start a whole new forest. If the fire were to be extinguished quickly, those seeds would never be released to become the next evolution. The old trees would rot and die without the new growth coming, and eventually the whole forest would stagnate and die. But the forest fire burns away the old trees, making room for the released seeds to take root and sprout, giving them enough sunlight and warmth to really thrive without being overshadowed by the thick canopy overhead. The earth is being replenished and renewed by the ashes, and so a whole new cycle of growth is the result.

In nature, this happens regularly: what appears as destruction on one level is also creating optimal conditions for the birth of something new, for evolution. In the same way, your problems, whether they are acute or chronic, are causing you to ask more meaningful questions, to develop capacities other than just putting on a Band-Aid. That problem must come back again in some form, usually becoming bigger and bigger until you have understood the deeper message and addressed the root cause.

It's only when a problem arises that is difficult, or impossible to solve, that we turn to the invisible Spirit and to prayer. The first reaction to any issue is always to fix it, to repair it, to resolve it on the material level: go to the doctor; talk to your boss; have it out with your partner; write to your senator. All those things may have to be done in due course, but the first thing to do is turn your attention to God. As you've already seen in the first chapter, we live in a perfect spiritual Universe of ideas and patterns, infinite and always unfolding in time. One of the mechanisms through which that perfection unfolds is contrast and challenge, or duality. And when you resist change, problems appear. That's only because the infinite perfection of Spirit is trying to unfold in your life, but you have a different idea. Spirit sees the bigger picture, knows the purpose for which it incarnated as you, and is trying to fulfill that purpose. You, in your human body, have lost sight of everything you knew when you were pure Spirit and are exercising your free will to attain the things your ego's limited awareness desires.

So you are dragged kicking and screaming through problems representing the gap between your ego's and your Spirit's perception, to your ultimate destiny. Your journey would be much easier if you released resistance to what appears and trusted in the wisdom of the

Universe. The closer your vibration comes to that of Spirit, the more you can grow through insights and revelation rather than problems. However, no one is ever completely immune from challenges; life keeps happening and even the great masters were faced with greater challenges than any other human being has ever had to face. So the more you understand and work with your problems, rather than resist them, the less suffering you create. It's never the issue in itself that causes suffering–it's your resistance to it.

A problem is a matter of interpretation. It's a judgment that arises in a mind that doesn't know everything is God. What you see as a problem is in some way a gift, a new possibility for an expansion of the character you are in this play that is your life. It's through overcoming challenges, facing and slaying the dragons, that you become strong, resilient, inventive, and empowered. To God, there are no problems. Things are what they are, without any judgment attached to them. It's your ego, knowing itself as separate from God, which has judgments about things. When they are inconvenient to the ego, not what it wants them to be, the judgment is "bad." When they are convenient, what it wants, the judgment is "good." To Spirit, things just are what they are: ice just is. To a figure skater, having ice is a good thing and he experiences happiness; to the person who can't use his car to get to work, ice is an upsetting experience. It is your judgment of a situation or event that makes it good or bad.

Perfection Exists in Everything

Perfection is a principle and resides in unity, meaning it's whole and complete. Humans reside in duality and think of perfection as "good," which really means convenient for them. In order to better understand a non-dualistic perception and to get away from judgment, consider this: every thought or feeling you have is a perfect example of having that exact thought or feeling.

THE POWER OF PROBLEMS: USING CHALLENGES TO MAKE YOU STRONGER

When we see things as imperfect, we are just confusing perfection with what we want. What looks imperfect to us may look perfect to someone else. Take even war atrocities: to the perpetrator, they were the right course of action. How we see things is a perception, but perfection is a principle. A possible way to see "bad" things as perfect is to realize they are perfect examples of whatever they are. So if I'm frustrated, that is a perfect expression of frustration: "I'm perfectly frustrated!"

Divinity is always working for you, not against you. If you can see an unwanted situation as a gift for your highest evolution, and just acknowledge and affirm it as a gift, then you suspend the need to look for how or why it's a gift. Whether you accept it or not is immaterial–the situation already is. So acknowledgement, rather than unwilling and difficult acceptance, takes all the pressure off. You can dislike it all you want, but it's a gift for your evolution.

So instead of beating yourself up for being unkind, unfeeling, or unspiritual, just accept that everything must be a perfect example of whatever it is. You being unkind in this moment is a perfect example of unkindness, and as a witness of that feeling you have created a small gap between you and the feeling. From that awareness you can then choose to have a kinder response than before, or a higher understanding of the situation.

Cultivating such a perception can free you of most, if not all the judgments you have about yourself, events, or situations. Just because you have a problem and are working on it does not stop you from remembering that ultimately, this is not the truth about you as Spirit. Work with the problem, not to try solving it, but to discover its real meaning, to find the greater potential awaiting you. Instead of asking Spirit to heal the issue, whether financial, relational, or anything else, you sincerely ask, "Show me what *I need to change* in my thoughts, beliefs, behavior, and activity in order for my issue to heal." Spirit will show you the answer. Start taking responsibility; you were the one who first created the imbalance in your body or your life, not willfully, but through ignorance. You are the only one who can un-create it.

God's creation that is all perfection is done, everything already exists but we don't see it all at once. We are only aware of events unfolding in time and space; we forget we created this experience–not the event, not the situation, but our experience of it - to feel it fully and release it, so the next experience can unfold. In the material world, we don't look through the eyes of God, but consider ourselves as someone separate from God. In fact, we are never separate from the spiritual world that is our Source; we just entertain a material sense of the wholeness of God.

We are like the blue, red, or green patches on the floor of a cathedral when the sun shines through a stained-glass window. We are different sizes and colors, but are an expression of the perfect, translucent light ray shining through our personal, cultural, and historical filters to make us the humans we are, appearing very different from each other. We seem to bear neither resemblance nor relation to that ray of light; yet without it, we would simply not exist. Without our filters, which are beliefs and judgments, we would just be pure white light–angelic beings.

Where we are now, in the world of duality or different colors, we are trying to understand this principle of oneness and perfection: our Source or the ray of light. Rather than seeking to unify the different colors, or different perspectives, we must forget about the good

> We are not on our way back to the sun, we are the rays carrying the qualities of the sun into the world through our personal filters, and illuminating everything we touch with beautiful individual colors.

and bad, the right and left, the up and down, and imagine a totally new nature of Reality where everything just IS. The colors from the stained-glass window falling on the floor are our present material reality. How can these colors have even an inkling of what the cause of them looks like? They would imagine a mixture of themselves that would always create new hues and colors, but wouldn't get them to understand the true Reality of the sunray. How do you imagine something you know nothing about?

In the same way, both the good and the bad of this world have nothing to do with the "IS-ness" or the nature of God, which is our true nature. The nature of light before it hits those filters has nothing to do with the colors that appear on the floor. They are a relative projection of the Divine perfection. We are not on our way back to the sun, we are the rays carrying the qualities of the sun into the world through our personal filters, and illuminating everything we touch with beautiful individual colors.

How to Consciously Work with Problems

Einstein said, "You cannot solve a problem with the level of thinking that created it."[1] So even science and physics admit there are levels of thinking that influence the solving of problems. A certain level of thought will keep the problem in place, while another level will likely dissolve it. Every level of thought is a frequency. As you change your thought, it becomes another frequency, influencing everything connected to it to become something different to some degree.

Based on the knowledge you have uncovered up to now, it would be logical to align yourself with the perspective of Source. The attributes of the mind of God differ from those of the human mind. In Spirit, there are no problems, while in human life they seem to prosper. So it would be logical to look at problems from a different angle, from the viewpoint of Spirit, and place them in the context of knowing that you have designed them for your highest good and quickest evolution.

Events, situations, and conditions will always exist in the world. They are what actually constitute a material world; however, they only become a problem when you identify with the ego and resist. If the ego doesn't get its own way, or thinks it's being disrespected or inconvenienced, it reacts, defends, or justifies itself. Once you remember that you are a spiritual being, unconditionally loved by the divine, and that everything is a gift from Spirit, you will know that everything you are experiencing must be for your ultimate good. Then you will start to perceive things differently and will gradually achieve a deeper and more conscious connection with divinity.

This doesn't mean you can't have that connection when life is good; but when all is well materially, you tend to forget about the deeper realities of life. When you quickly solve small problems, without needing a spiritual consciousness, you tend to forget that all solutions emerge from your Divinity. It's only when a problem arises that seems impossible to solve by material means that we are forced to dig deeper and make a connection with that Presence of God, the truth of our being. From this higher level of thinking, new and untried perspectives or insights will become available.

Challenges Make You Grow

Review all the issues you uncovered so far, just globally. Remember what you worked on in the last chapter, whatever the issue was for you. Look at the shadows you have discovered of being selfish, a failure, a fraud, weak, worthless, incapable . . . and how working with them in the shadow exercise has helped you see their real value. They allowed you to develop qualities, abilities, or a talent you really appreciate now. Just bring all that to mind again, and see who you have become because of those challenges.

THE POWER OF PROBLEMS: USING CHALLENGES TO MAKE YOU STRONGER

And it's not only challenges that assist and support you, but also all events that happened–the box of magic tricks you received for Christmas when you were eight that made you so excited to show off the tricks you learned, first to your family, then to your friends. Eventually, you performed better tricks at parties and sometimes even got paid for it! That started your career as a magician. So everything in life is conspiring for your good, showing you possibilities; and if they resonate, are exciting, if you love doing something, then practice it, work with it until it becomes yours.

If it's a challenge that appears, instead of lamenting, "What have I done to deserve this" or "Why is this happening to me," start asking questions such as "What's the real meaning of this experience? Is there a hidden possibility or something new that could be explored?" Then tap into your intuition, the messages Spirit sends you through the mind. The message of Spirit can very easily get distorted when it has to go through the filters of the ego. When you are afraid of going broke, of a health challenge, of being abandoned, remember you now have a higher awareness and that this fear is just Spirit trying to inspire you to make positive changes in your life. Become aware that Spirit is who you are, and you are always safe.

Any message from Spirit must be a loving one, since it is all love; anything that sparks a fearful reaction, one that is less than love, must be a misinterpretation of something that was designed for your higher evolution. Your problem just needs to be reinterpreted into the real message your Consciousness has sent you–one that is loving, respectful, validating, and elevates your frequency.

Doing this helps us to contextualize, to reframe our approach to problems that are subjective; to Spirit, the event just IS. A problem is always relative to *your* situation, *your* circumstances, and *your* mindset. It always has to do with the physical, temporal you.

For example, imagine the electricity suddenly goes off in your house. It feels like disaster to the person on their computer who has just lost three hours' work on their project; it's mildly upsetting to the housewife who's cooking dinner for her family, but disaster again if she has eight guests coming for dinner in about an hour. I know, it has happened to me! But if you happen to be reading a book in daytime, it's no big deal–you might not even notice; and if it's evening, you light a few candles and enjoy the changed atmosphere. If you're out on a walk, you don't even know it happened. The event is what it is; your experience is what you make of it in any given circumstance.

If your partner decides to leave you, if you're involved in an accident, or if you lose your job, it's your interpretation of the event that makes you happy or unhappy, apprehensive or hopeful. Negative thoughts–such as *I don't deserve this, they're always criticizing me, I never get what I want*–keep you in victim mode, while empowering questions unlock the hidden gift within the problem. So ask, "What's the larger vision, or version of me that's trying to emerge because of this?" Interpret your problem in the context of a greater potential seeking to emerge. You need to move from being just a problem-solver to a vision-holder, and to see a larger context, a higher possibility. Then from that more expanded place you keep asking more questions, such as "What is the more expansive life I could now start? What's that greater purpose? How is this serving me? What can I learn? How can I be of service?" We are not living our lives just for ourselves; we are all in a larger context of service to everyone else.

Our Universe Is a Visible Expression of Invisible Energy

The whole Universe, including us, is an infinite ocean of energy, expressing in visibility as all the things we see, all interdependent in some way. That ocean is expressing as wavelets that come smoothing out a beach, or as bigger waves sculpting the rocks into caves and caverns, or as the mist rising from it under the influence of the sun. Some of the mist never moves very far and falls right back into the ocean, only to rise again. That can represent the angelic realms. The mist that rises and moves farther away forms denser clouds that represent the visible realm; every drop in those clouds represents a human being or some other part of creation. The clouds are carried by winds over the lands to become rain, and every drop, wherever it falls, carries all the life-giving qualities to the rest of God's world.

Some drops fall on beaches, quickly and easily making their way back to the ocean, to again rise to form new clouds. Others fall over deserts, where they are absorbed to form invisible, underground rivers that feed oases. Sometimes a heavy cloud breaks over a forest, and the drops wash the dust off the leaves before feeding the roots, making vegetation grow, carrying sap into the branches and foliage. Some drops fall into mountain streams making them into rivers, providing water for thirsty creatures of all kinds. Others fall on tops of mountains as snow, giving nature time to rest and sleep before melting and starting up the cycle of growth again in the spring. Every drop is essential to the well-being of nature exactly where it is. It may take some time for a drop to get back to the ocean, depending on its function. The drop that got absorbed by the roots of an apple tree had to transform into the sap that became the flower, then the fruit, which became the nourishment for some part of life.

In the same way, every human being has his own purpose and function in the world, and each one is absolutely necessary to the wholeness of life. Some people that seem to have easy and smooth lives are like the drops falling on a beach. Others, like the drops over deserts that form underground rivers, are people not in the public eye. They are never on TV shows, are invisible and quiet–but they live their full potential as an inspiration and support to everyone who touches their lives. And still others have difficult lives, go through many transformations, but they all end up in the same place, back with Source. Just as each drop after many changes of form will rejoin the ocean, so will each person, regardless of their trials and tribulations, consciously come back to the realization of their oneness with God.

Every path in life is different from every other path, but each person is unique and essential for the transformation and well-being of everything that lies within their consciousness. If you are having a difficult time, it all serves a purpose you may not be aware of right now. Your final destination is guaranteed; yet unlike the drops that fall where the wind has taken them, we have free will that will determine the path we take towards our destination. In this way predestination and free will are not mutually exclusive. Predestination is Unity with Spirit and is a given, is guaranteed. But the way to get there is dictated by our free will. Also, unlike the raindrops, we can never be separate from Source, since Source contains within itself all the component parts of this metaphor: the ocean, the sun, the winds, and the lands. Our sense of separation from each other, from nature, and from Source is imagined; it's just a perception.

Material Problems Get Resolved through Spiritual Focus

Problems are not necessary for your growth; you could live a happy, joyful, and abundant life focusing on spiritual evolution, service to others, and grow, as the Scriptures say, "Unto him be glory… world without end. (Ephesians 3:21) But the unfortunate fact is that when we have all we desire materially, we forget about Spirit and that our abundance and happiness comes from there. As Jonathan Bender once said to me, "Comfort creates complacency."[2] Our focus becomes materialistic. When small problems appear, and we try to solve them on their surface level without changing our perception, they grow into bigger and bigger ones. Problems only exist in the material world, but they get resolved through our focus on the spiritual one. To experience a world with no sense of a problem, we must first know the Truth that we are spiritual beings beyond the world. We are not in the world–but the world is in our Consciousness.

Problems Are Showing Us Opportunities

Do you have issues in areas of health, finances, relationships, or work? Do you need to give more attention to your personal development, to being of service, to your spirituality? Are you being that five-year-old, overreacting to the present situation?

Whatever your particular problem may be right now, whether a health challenge, a financial loss, or a fight with your spouse, bring your attention to what might be seeking to emerge through that problem. What qualities of being or feeling are missing? Trust, confidence, decisiveness, generosity, being outgoing, authentic? Notice how this involves a shift in your perception, from your negative feelings to positive elements that could stem from your issue. And it will require some action to really ground those new aspects of your being.

Just imagine if your rent was due in a week, and you simply didn't have the money! Your salary would only come at the end of the month. Negotiating with the owner didn't work, and you can see yourself living in your car soon. You can either sink into despair, or make a conscious effort to think thoughts such as these: "Since I have this situation, it must be for my ultimate good. I don't have to know how, but I know it will be. With my next salary I will budget my expenses more carefully; since I will live in my car, there will be no more rent to pay. Lots of free parking spaces at night. I have a friend who will be dog-sitting all next month, and will ask her if I can shower and wash my clothes there." You are no longer quite as despondent because your vibration has lifted a little bit, and you can see some short-term hope.

You also prepare for the inevitable by collecting cartons and clearing some stuff you don't really need. Then you phone your friend with the intention of telling her of your predicament and asking about showering at her place. Before you even start, she launches into how her mother is sick, how she has to leave to look after her, and can't take that dog-sitting job where she's supposed to be at the end of the week. Your spirits slump again. It seems you'll have to find a different solution for your problem! But you compassionately listen and finally hear that your friend wants someone to dog-sit instead of her. Of course, you offer your help. You'll now have an eternally grateful friend as well as a place to live for a month, and extra money in addition to your salary. All this lifts your frequency even more, and you know that a better, more permanent solution will show up when this month is finished. You don't have to know what that might be, but you can now trust.

Out of the problem of not having enough money, a new you has grown: one who consciously keeps her thoughts in the highest register possible, prepares for any eventuality, and keeps her eyes open for avenues from which help can come. Any judgments you once had about yourself or your situation have now evaporated and in this new vibration, more and better solutions can keep showing up.

Problems Help You Evolve

Now look at your own problem to find the blessings. How is this problem a way for you to evolve? How is it an opportunity for you to become more patient, more tolerant, more giving, wiser? How can it help you become more creative, more independent, firm in your attitude, more harmonious? How can you become more discerning, courageous, resilient, accepting when you're faced with a fact that can't be changed. How do you find a new perspective?

When you seem to be lacking something, you must start giving that very thing or quality out, because, in the words of Derek Rydall, "What you're missing is what you are not giving."[3] If you feel unappreciated, disrespected, not valued, it's because you are not respecting, appreciating, or valuing yourself or others. Since you can't give what you don't have, first find appreciation and respect for yourself before extending it to others. Even when you seem to be lacking money, the same principle applies. You must start giving, however little, even a dollar to a beggar in the street, with the consciousness of "I have this to give" so the Universe can respond with more of the things you're giving. It's your consciousness of "having," whether abilities, talents, money, intelligence, or whatever else, which draws to you more of what you declare you have and give.

Even if you're bedridden, take that as having time for rest and reflection instead of being frustrated about all the things you cannot do. When you lose your job, view that as an opportunity to start refining the project you never had time to really develop. Be willing to think outside the narrow box you've been in, and ask yourself what would you just love to do, now that you can choose. Everything that happens can become an opportunity to trust that the divine answers our prayers in spite of appearances to the contrary; we just have to be willing to look, and take one step towards our goal. Remember the money hidden in the attic: John had been nudged many times to make that garage sale before he was laid off, but found reasons not to listen. Finally, the Universe had to find a way to make him do it.

If gentle ways don't work, painful ones usually will.

Any change in a situation requires a shift in perspective first, and then some action. When you think life is unfair, you're badly treated, or just not getting your way, resistance sets in and you have a fight on your hands. In the long run, this never works. Instead, first look for a more expanded view. Place yourself at the level of Spirit where nothing is a problem. Consider other ideas on the best way to deal with the present situation. Achieve internal peace first; only then taking the action that seems best. Wishing the situation wasn't there, or was different, is, to say the least, unproductive.

You might want to find the deeper reason for this situation, and so I invite you to close your eyes and follow along in this exercise, developed by my mentor, Derek Rydall, taking you along the timeline of your life.

TIMELINE EXERCISE

Once again, look at your concerns, find the biggest one you have in this moment, or the issue that is the most difficult for you, and mentally ask, *What is it trying to tell me in the area of my health, relationships, finances*, whatever that might be. As you focus beyond just the material hurt or pain, the inconvenience or anxiety, what begins to come up? What is it trying to tell you about your beliefs, your fears, or about the way you perceive life? What's the hidden higher potential or possibility of expansion within it? Who is the larger *you* trying to emerge?

Then switch from your mind to emotions: How does the present situation make you feel? What do you feel about your problem? Is it anxiety, anger, or shame? Do you feel unsupported, betrayed, or worthless? Are you afraid, frustrated, or humiliated? And now start taking deep breaths, each one deeper than the last. Inhale deeply into your abdomen, keeping your attention on the base of your spine. Breathe in the Light you are always surrounded by, and breathe out everything that no longer serves you. Feel a calmness descend upon you.

Now imagine there is a timeline above you that stretches from your past to the present moment and on into the future, and see yourself rise up above that into the timeless. Envision yourself above the timeline in the present, and get in touch again with that feeling you had down below, either the chronic emotion or most painful, limiting belief, whatever it was—"I am incapable, unworthy, not good enough, a failure." Feel that sense of hopelessness, bitterness, and desperation. What's the most intense feeling about your problem?

You are now floating above your timeline, safely away from the problem below that's in your present. Allow yourself to fully experience your emotion, because it is now safe to feel that. Allow your feeling to grow more intense. In a little while, you will move backward along the timeline to when you first felt this emotion. Pass all the other times when it has been reinforced by similar events, and return to that first time you felt it. In a moment, you'll do that.

But now, you are hovering right above your body and feeling the emotion. You see yourself down below. Observe the pattern all these successive emotions have traced in your brain and your body. Study that pattern from up above, seeing it light up more and more as you intensify your feelings. Know you are safe, your spirit is in charge, and that its innate wisdom guides and protects you during this entire exploration.

And now, you begin to move back along the timeline, pulled by this emotion that wants to go home, to the place where it was born. You are going faster and faster, trusting your spirit will guide you to exactly where you need to be, to the moment when you first felt this emotion. Let yourself be drawn there, and, without any thought, just drop down into that place and look around. Notice other people who may be there. Notice how old you are, what you are doing, what you are feeling. It may be just flashes of memories or incomplete pictures. You are the observer of what is happening. Who's there? How does it feel? Just observe.

Now you can rise back out of that event, above the timeline again, higher and higher, and move back about an hour before that event. It has not yet taken place, so you don't have that emotion yet. Rise even higher until the timeline is almost invisible down below. You feel connected to Source and understand everything that happens has a purpose beyond what appears. You, as Spirit, have created this event so your human personality, down below the timeline, could overcome it, could use its free will to see the perspective of Source and express its qualities into the world.

Recognize that this event has helped you grow in some way, discover something new, learn to stand in your power, or be more tolerant, confident, and generous. Maybe it has changed the direction your life was going to better serve your own life purpose and be of service to others. Whatever it is, there is always a deeper reason for every trauma, every issue, and every problem.

You are now very close to your Source, high above the human timeline. Here, you are willing and able to remember and see why you created that experience. Your vision is expanding and your heart is opening. You know this was for the evolution of your character, so you could fulfill your soul's purpose to bring your gifts to the world. You can feel your crown chakra opening. The tingling sensation is the energy and the wisdom of Spirit flooding into you, allowing you to see exactly why it created this particular event, how it has helped your evolution, and what you are to express through your life.

If you have had a health challenge, perhaps it has pushed you into developing a way to help others through similar difficulties. If you have been experiencing lack and limitation, perhaps it has steered you on a journey to discover the true source of abundance, so you would never again lack for anything and could teach others to do the same.

Your Higher Self is now filling you with its wisdom, even if it doesn't come through as words. It may come as a feeling, an inspiration, a knowing. It fills your whole body and leaves no room for any limiting or false beliefs, any negative emotions or thoughts, or any erroneous perceptions to remain in your field. They are all being swept out of your consciousness and out of your body. You feel how this divine energy detoxifies and cleanses you. You are renewed and energized. Take a deep breath, anchoring that feeling in your body.

You are your Spirit. As you take another deep breath, you float down towards your timeline and that original event. You radiate the energy of who you are now from your heart, through your hands and your eyes, saturating the event with it. When you float lower, you recognize that the negative charge has disappeared and has been replaced with the wisdom, confidence, love, and joy that you emanate at this moment.

Rise up again out of this event and move forward along the timeline, still carrying within you all the wisdom, understanding, and clear vision of what life is really about that you discovered when you were with your Source. As you notice old perceptions or stressful events connected to that original event coming up, you radiate the new energy you now carry over them, and watch as they disintegrate in the light of the love from your heart blessing them.

Now as you reach the point where you are in the present, take a deep breath and slowly sink back into your timeline, letting the ripple effect of all you've done stabilize into your new reality. You feel that with your new insights and understanding, your whole history has changed. You are no longer the same person who was playing the part of your character before, no longer the victim, the weak, incapable, or unworthy character. With the understanding you have gathered, the gift you have received of seeing the bigger picture, having compassion for every painful situation or circumstance, and everything you have learned, you can now truly become the creator of your future life, as you want it to be.

Rest in this moment of empowerment. Take a few deep breaths and feel grateful for all that has been revealed, for the reclaiming of your real identity. Feel confident that from this moment on, whatever challenges come up for you–as they will–you will remember that you are the hero of the play you have scripted for yourself to triumph over all obstacles and attain new heights of Being. Every passing day you will become more like the Spirit you truly are.

You Can Achieve What You Want

You, and no one else, have total responsibility for your life, since you have been given free will to choose your course of action. Whether you use it with integrity, compassion, and for the highest good of all as Spirit would use it, or with just your personal comfort and abundance in mind, this is a choice you make in every moment of your life.

If your circumstances are not what you like, it's not God punishing you for some wrongdoing. They are the result of your past thoughts, beliefs, and actions that were incongruent with what Spirit is, and of your identification with the ego. More simply, we call them "good" or "bad" choices.

If you've made a bad choice, it's OK because you've now realized it and can make a better one next time a challenge appears. You have

THE POWER OF PROBLEMS: USING CHALLENGES TO MAKE YOU STRONGER

learned a lesson, discovered the deeper reason for that particular challenge, which helped you evolve to become a better human being. Additionally, you have discovered the potential for some growth in that challenge and have become your own savior. The answers you've been looking for outside of yourself have always been in you, right where you are, in every aspect of your life. All you need to do is use every appearance, reframe every event, especially the unwanted ones, to find the divine perspective within every situation.

You do that by realizing that everything is energy; both science and spirituality tell you that. Energy is not good or bad–it just IS. So there is no bad or evil energy. If you look at the principle of Truth, there is no good and no evil. There is only energy, the quantum field, the Source; however, what you direct this energy to do is a whole different thing. Energy or Source is whole, complete, infinite, eternal, and perfect, meaning there is nothing outside of it or other than it. The truth of all energy is perfection or love, regardless of what it looks like or what people have done to us, and irrespective of everything that has happened in the world. What people do with energy and how they use it through ignorance or willfulness has nothing to do with what energy is.

> The answers you've been looking for outside of yourself have always been in you, right where you are.

To honor that omnipresent energy, you start by loving yourself *as* that energy, which means respecting yourself, claiming all that you are, knowing you are a part of the whole, then loving and honoring everything else as part of the same energy.

Bad Choices Are Also Good Choices

Of course, you never make a "bad" choice on purpose—so you must have been ignorant of something, or had some beliefs that were either not true or limiting. Discover what beliefs were hiding in the situation and set about changing them. When you do the work of introspection, you will realize how you can get your life back on track where you want it to be. Since you know energy and all the goodness of divinity is everywhere, it's also where you are. If it is not apparent in your life, you must have somehow blocked it.

Just as water does not come through a twisted garden hose even when it's turned on completely, the fullness of Spirit does not flow through you and into your world until you have untwisted and straightened out the kinks in your beliefs.

We have already seen the only control you have is over your own thoughts and actions. Those are the only things you can change; in the long run, it is useless to try and change outside circumstances. Until you shift your internal perceptions, unwanted external circumstances will continue to show up in one form or another. Your connection to your soul is your GPS—God Positioning System, as Derek Rydall calls it—and will course-correct you if you have taken a wrong turn. But you don't sit in your driveway, even when you've given all the directions to your GPS, and expect it to tell you how to get to your destination. You have to start moving for that to happen. If you're parked someplace, it will never tell you anything. And it will never tell you all the turns to take at once. Your GPS will give you just one step at a time, and when you've taken it, it will tell you the next step. Occasionally, perhaps you'll hear, "Turn around when possible!" which just means that you have strayed off your path.

Based on the potentials you may have discovered from your problems so far and your life story, you can now see what's been trying to emerge; see your real vision and purpose. Basically, all your Source wants is for you is to be happy and fulfilled. This has to be broken down into its material components, so go for the things that make you happy and fulfilled and are in service to others as well. Without that service component you can never be really fulfilled. As stated in *Conversations with God* by Neale Donald Walsch, "Your life is not about you; it has to do with everyone whose lives you touch, and the way in which you touch them."[4] I had disregarded my GPS many times—and it kept signaling, each signal stronger than the last—until I was forced to surrender. I am always being course-corrected and do my best to listen before it gets too painful. Don't wait until your signals get painful and disruptive; stay alert and open to the growth process that shows new possibilities at every turn.

Choose Your Priorities and Work Them Relentlessly

Your goals, desires, and dreams evolve alongside your growth. What you want will change, but always for something even better, even grander than you could have imagined. However, don't be a weathercock pointing to a different direction whenever you hit a threshold or a difficulty. Difficulties arise so you can overcome them; they are not the Universe saying you are not meant to have this or that. After all, when the lights go off in your house, and all the other houses on the street have light, do you interpret it as you're not supposed to have light? Or do you become resourceful, change the fuse or call in an electrician?

Take the time to discover your deepest real desire and make it a priority in your life. Then stay with it; commit to making it work in spite of difficulties that arise—because they will—for at least a year or eighteen months. If you're committed and do your best, it must work. You are that omnipotent, omniscient Spirit that wants your happiness. So stay connected to your GPS and trust the corrections it makes to your journey. You will arrive at the destination you ultimately want, even if it doesn't look quite same as the one you envisioned in the beginning. Yet this is the one you now want, and it's the one Spirit wants for you. Your goal, and your Spirit's goal, have become one.

Review of chapter 4:
- ❖ Within every problem or issue lies the solution to that problem, which is first, elevating your consciousness, and second, developing God-qualities you are still lacking.
- ❖ Problems just show you where you are out of alignment with Spirit.
- ❖ To uncover the gift that lies in every issue that appears becomes the solution.

CHAPTER 5

THE POWER OF MANIFESTATION: GETTING WHAT YOU REALLY WANT

*I*magine that you want some fruit—and just suppose there are no grocery stores in your world as yet. But you know that every kind of fruit imaginable grows in Napa Valley. Well, not quite, but you know what I mean; you have apples, pears, grapes, peaches, nectarines, and plums. . . everything is there. So where do you go when you want apples? To Napa Valley. And if you want peaches, where do you go? To Napa Valley. Whatever you want, you will always find there. The valley is very large, has many orchards, and you don't really know where to find the pears that you came to get. You meet some other people wandering around looking for what they want, so ask them if they saw some pears anywhere. They give you directions, which may or may not turn out correct because maybe what they saw from a distance and thought were pears were, in fact, green apples.

You realize that wandering around and asking the people you meet for directions hasn't, so far, helped you arrive where you want to be, and that you have to find the head gardener and ask him, since he knows where everything is, and knows the best and quickest way to get exactly what you need. It may take you a little time to locate the head gardener; but once you have made contact with him, asked your question, and listened to and applied his directions, you will go straight to your goal without getting lost on the way.

What if I told you that not only do you have the power to get what you really want, but also you have the power to manifest in ways that defy the laws of nature and physics? I will get back to that in a little while, but first, let's briefly review what we have discovered so far.

First, we established the fundamentals of life that there's one power, which is everywhere and therefore must be where you are, because of Oneness. You must be it, and wherever you are is where the power is. Whenever you think you're separate from the one power, that's when you give all your power away to people, things, and conditions; you identify with the body, the material conditions, and that is the first great power leak.

Then we looked at the implications of this. You cannot access this power, which is inherently yours, until you move from being a victim to full personal responsibility; and the deepest sense of personal responsibility is the ability, through free will, to choose your responses, your focus, what you pay attention to, what you believe, and how you perceive events.

The next step is how to begin making this change, and that entails going deeper and being really honest with where you stand. You did the work of becoming aware and responsible, and it has uncovered all the relative conditions, filters, and beliefs that have been keeping you powerless. These are all your little power leaks, stemming from the first big power leak.

Then you discovered that within your core problems there are potentials for growth, and working with this creates a healing. You learned to embrace and integrate the parts of you that were unwanted and unseen. Based on everything discovered so far, you began to really get a sense of the life that's trying to emerge through you. You had a glimpse of what a life living your full power might really look like.

THE POWER OF MANIFESTATION: GETTING WHAT YOU REALLY WANT

But in order to live the life you want, you have to move out of being merely a problem solver into being a vision holder. That's where you start asking, "What do I really want?"

What You Really Want

You want to have success in your life. An ideal partner, enough money to live without worries, take your family on vacation, have your dream job. Or be in good health, get a house, a boat, or your own business—all legitimate desires, but not all achievable right now. You know all manifestation starts in the mind, and mostly unknowingly, you have manifested the reality you are in now. Unknowingly, because you would never have wanted to manifest something you don't like. If there are things you don't like in your life, and you know from the previous chapters that you are the creator of your reality, then you realize there is a disconnect somewhere that you're not aware of. Otherwise, you could not have created what you don't want.

EXERCISE

Let's take some time right now to think of all the things that you want in life. On a piece of paper, write down all the large and small things you desire. So for example, you want your health or vitality back. You want to lose weight. You want the ideal partner, or to buy a house, a boat, or have a garden. You want to win the lottery, to have success, the job of your dreams, to grow orchids, to have a child, write a book, be a race-car driver . . . just fill in the blank for yourself.

There are so many things you want and haven't achieved yet, and, so far, wishing for them and making affirmations and vision-boards hasn't worked. And although manifestation starts in the mind, where possibilities have been substantially dormant, they're still not visible! So what's missing is the particular feeling of *coming* from a place where you know they are already yours, so they can manifest. I want to stress the fact that you can't have or keep any material thing unless you become that rich or healthy person within your consciousness. Even if you manage to regain vitality through taking medications, you will just manifest another kind of lack of health.

But becoming a house, your partner, or "success" is at best vague or downright impossible. So what do you *really* wish for when you want all those things you've just written down?

Now I invite you to take another page, and we will do an exercise to make you realize the difference between what you want, and what you *really* want.

Divide that new page into two columns. Call the first column "Things I want" and the second column "Why I want them." In the left-hand column, under "Things I want," write out what you want in life. Look at that list of things you made a minute ago, and, just for the sake of time, take only a few of all those things that you think would make you happy, joyful, and fulfilled. You can look at the rest of your items later, and do the same exercise for every one of them. For now, write a few, one under the other, in the left-hand column, leaving some space in between. The right-hand column is

> Realize the difference between what you want, and what you really want.

for the reasons why you want each thing–but if the reason is material, add that to your "Things I want" column, and keep asking why you want that, until you get down to some quality, rather than a material thing. So only qualities go in the right-hand column.

For example, if your first item is "money" and the reason for wanting it is because you want to buy a house, "house" will go under the "Things I want" heading. Now think why you want a house. Maybe you'd like to have more space, more rooms, so "space" or "rooms" will again go under the "Things I want" heading, and now you think of why you want more space. If it's to make you comfortable, then "comfort" is what you really desire, and that will go into the right-hand "Why" column.

Or if you want a speedboat, why do you want a speedboat? If it's so that people appreciate and admire you, that is still not the real "why" because it's dependent on getting something from outside of you. That also goes under the "Things I want" heading because you want admiration from others. Now reflect on why do you want people to admire or appreciate you? Is it because you want to *feel* loved and respected, or you want to *feel* free and adventurous, and that is the real reason for wanting that speedboat?

Do this process with every item on your list, and you will end up with a list of qualities or feelings you want to have. Those are the things you really want, and the material things will become easier to achieve once the qualities are anchored in you. What's more, you're no longer dependent on someone else for achieving your desires: realize that nothing, and nobody except yourself can ever give you those feelings. You generate them from inside of you, regardless of what your circumstances may be–because remember, you have all the qualities of Source within you, dormant until you activate those you most want. Fill yourself up with them, and when you're feeling capable, peaceful, happy, or whatever else, that will flow out into your world, giving joy, appreciation, comfort, and love to all around you.

You must take charge of your human mind. Become more aware of what Spirit has in its mind for you, through consciously connecting with your Spirit. Remember, you may not always get what you want, but you will always get what you need for your highest evolution.

Activate the Qualities of Your Vision

Now that you've discovered what you really want, and before you have the abundance or ability to satisfy your material desires, you can start by activating the qualities you came up with in your life. They are the very substance of your continued growth. Introduce objects into your home that make you feel happy, peaceful, or abundant. Meet with people who are fun and joyful more often, and avoid those who irritate or upset you. Stop looking at the depressing news on TV. Activate the qualities you want present in your life, and as you do that, one by one, the material things seem to appear. Other times you find you no longer want them, because different things have now become your priorities. Introducing qualities into your life doesn't need to strain your budget, it only requires changing some of your habits, and acting as if you were that generous, confident, or abundant person. Hold yourself straighter, give some coins to the street musician with a smile and a word of thanks; if you want to live healthier, buy organic food, but perhaps a little less so you don't actually spend more. As a bonus, you might even become slimmer!

You may also want to look at what people, places, and things make you feel the opposite of those qualities, and start engineering those out of your life. This might be a little more difficult where people are concerned, but just start seeing a little less of them than you did previously. Don't accept every invitation; give yourself some space. You don't have to do it all at once, but gradually remove the things that don't serve you. Slowly build a plan for how you would want your life to look. The plan will include the people, places, and environments you decide to have around you, and then you combine that with the practical actions necessary to implement your visionary goal. Those will, of course, be very different for everyone, so you must find all the elements and qualities best fitted to your unique path in this lifetime. As you practice and keep doing this work, your overall frequency will rise higher and higher, your body and affairs will reflect this and feel and appear better. There is no end to what you can become, because your soul is infinite.

> There is no end to what you can become, because your soul is infinite.

Manifest What You Want

You can manifest anything–if it is congruent with your life purpose. Here's the story of how I once manifested a flower.

I had been given a plant that bloomed absolutely beautiful flowers in July and August. Since I was always in the United States from early May till some time in September, the friend who looked after my plants got to see those amazing flowers, while I never did. One day, I decided that I absolutely wanted to see them myself. As soon as the new growth started, I talked to the plant while watering it. I asked it to give me just one flower before I was due to leave on May 9. For two months, I really connected with my plant, giving it love and asking to see its flowers. Believe it or not, at end of April, one stalk produced a bud so small that I couldn't believe it would open up within two weeks. So I encouraged it daily to fully open into a flower before I left. On the morning of May 8, it was there: a full, white, beautiful flower on its stalk, when other buds were only barely appearing.

And just think what could have happened if I had not limited myself to asking for one flower. We so often limit ourselves by asking for what we think is possible, or reasonable, what doesn't put undue pressure on others. For Spirit, there is nothing that is more difficult than anything else. Spirit knows no limits. With a higher understanding, I could have had that whole plant covered in flowers. But for the human mind, steps are necessary to advance in consciousness, and each step leads to the next one.

Notice also that I had no preference for that flower to be any particular way; it didn't have to be white or pink, big or small, this shape or that. I just wanted to see the full beauty of that plant, whatever it was. To manifest, your only attachment must be to the feeling your experience will give you, letting go of any pictures you might have as to how it must look or be.

Live in a State of Gratitude

The easiest way to connect with Spirit is by your attention, gratitude, and appreciation for everything it has given you from birth, including your very life. You have all its attributes in potential, just as a seed holds its leaves and flowers in potential, but only expresses them when planted and allowed to grow. You have been planted in this world, have grown, and have the possibility to express whatever you wish through your choices. Let your vision for this lifetime, and the things you love to do, determine your actions, and be grateful for everything that appears, whether wanted or unwanted. It's always a gift, but sometimes the wrapping is not so great. See through the wrapping to the real gift.

THE POWER OF MANIFESTATION: GETTING WHAT YOU REALLY WANT

To manifest experiences to be grateful for, we must live in a state of gratitude. A happy experience only shows up because we've already activated gratitude somewhere along the line. An abundant experience is showing up because a consciousness of abundance has been activated in you sometime, someplace. As you practice feeling the qualities just discovered in the exercise of "Things I want," they will get clothed in visible form and begin to take shape according to your unique pattern. They will be as good, or better, than you imagined; they might also be different. That's why you must not be attached to a specific outcome, but rather to the feeling-tone. When you're attached to a specific visible picture of how it would look in your life, things might go wrong, change, or be taken away. But you can never go wrong by becoming attached to the feelings of peace, joy, wisdom, beauty, or abundance. They can manifest in countless different forms. The thing to do is create a way of life that allows them into your reality.

Let's explore one of the ways to do that, through bringing to mind, every night as you go off to sleep, all the good things that have happened this day or week. Explore not only things that have happened, but also things that you have achieved, things you are able to do or have done, and all of your successes.

Doing this as a written exercise at night has the additional value of anchoring within you the high frequencies of love, appreciation, and gratitude that will keep vibrating in your body for hours on end, without any interference from the lower vibrations generated by the challenging situations of everyday life.

EXERCISE

Start by being grateful for all the things you have materially, mentally, or emotionally: the comfort of your bed; the roof over your head; your money, even if it seems little; a job; the intelligence that allows you to keep it; love in your life from family, friends, or a pet; and a refrigerator full of food. You also have a telephone, a computer, eyesight, two arms and legs . . . there is no end to the good things you have when you start detailing them.

You also have a lot of things you don't actually own, but that are such a blessing. You have electricity running your appliances, public roads, and a sewage system. All of the knowledge you need is available through the Internet or public libraries. You are far richer than many of the rulers of ancient times, because you live in a home equipped with toasters, washers, dryers, and dishwashers, which is equivalent to a house full of servants.

Remember all the things you have ever achieved, all your successes. Learning your multiplication table, getting your degree, finding the love of your life. Depending on circumstances, getting out of bed or getting dressed might be an achievement. Focus on what you are able to do. You can create a project. You're able to write an article, paint, or play music, and you can build within yourself the inner feeling of achieving what you desire, which is the foundation of the actual material thing.

Be grateful for every small abundance as it appears. There are many people who do not have those things, or the abilities you have developed. Be grateful for all the things that so far you have taken for granted. Focus on all the good things, so that more of them can flow into your life. The Universe will always bring into your experience more of the things that match your frequency. If you continually worry, the Universe says, "You're always doing that. You must like it, so let's bring you more worries!" To the angry person it says, "Let's bring you more experiences that will anger you!" Whatever you are feeling, "Let's bring you more things that make you feel like that!" Life really is that simple, but it's not always easy to achieve.

How to Bring Your Vision into the World

Spirit hears your every prayer and desire and answers instantly, but you only experience the answer when your frequency comes close to that of Spirit. When your desire stems from a feeling of not having the thing you want, it has a frequency of lack or limitation. This is not congruent with the frequency of Spirit that knows no such thing as lack or limitation. Spirit IS all things, therefore cannot *not* be something. That is why Jesus said, "Whatsoever ye shall ask in prayer, believing, ye shall receive." (Matthew 21:22) And here, "believing" means believing it is already so. Just start imagining what it would be like to have what you want, to drive that car, to live in that house. Keep coming back to this every time you feel sad or despondent about your desire.

This means your focus is constantly being brought back to the life you want to live, and you are giving yourself the time to feel into how it would be to really live in that way. Activating the *feeling* and *being* qualities of your vision leads to the *doing* that will bring it into your life.

So first, allow yourself to really feel that life you envision and bask in it. Give a name to this feeling. Is it joyful, powerful, secure, harmonious, or supported? What else? What more? Once you have identified and perhaps written down the qualities you would be feeling, ask yourself, *Which people, places, or objects when I'm around them make me feel like that*? Then you'll know what you're *doing* must look like when engineering more of those people, places, and things into your life.

Then also ask yourself, *When I'm with those people, or in those places, who am I being?* Are you being outgoing, confident, generous, more helpful, or considerate? And again, your work now is to start *acting as if* you were that generous or outgoing person in your daily life. To be really clear on what you have to do, ask yourself, *What would it look like, specifically, to be, say, more generous or more confident?* Identify some practice or some action you could take such as being more generous with your time, your talent, or your money. Embrace expressing your truth rather than withholding it. Assist someone when they don't feel up to their task.

Even if some physical law seems to be standing in the way of manifesting your vision, know that physical laws don't override spiritual laws–and as the Bible says, "You have given him dominion over the works of your hands." (Psalms 8:6) Here, the word *him* can be interpreted as "man" so that we, as spiritual beings, have control over physical manifestation. The more you know yourself as Spirit, the more spiritual laws will take precedence over material laws until you begin to live a life that seems to be filled with miracles, large or small, rather than challenges.

Manifestation of Desire Depends on Your Frequency

Knowing you are your soul and connecting with Spirit must be an ongoing, consistent practice. As you raise your frequency, your desires start manifesting–or you no longer need or desire that thing. As soon as something we want manifests, we immediately start to want something else, never realizing how many of our desires are fulfilled.

THE POWER OF MANIFESTATION: GETTING WHAT YOU REALLY WANT

EXERCISE

Try the following exercise to really become aware of how many things you actually do manifest. First, write out a list of the things you would like to have right now, those that just don't seem possible, either because you can't afford them, or because they depend on the agreement of other people not willing to give it, or because it's not the policy of the company, or whatever. Once you have it, fold it over and put it away someplace where you're likely to forget it, at least for a while. Tuck it in the bottom of a bottom drawer or in a file you hardly ever open such as your taxes that you only look at every year. Find a place where you would come across it at some point, a year or two away. If you find your list sooner than a year, commit to not looking at it.

I've done it, and I had eleven items on my list. They seemed really impossible things to get or achieve. I had completely forgotten about my list, and it surfaced two (or more!) years later when I emptied a cluttered drawer. I hadn't put a date on my list, so didn't really know how long it had been since I had written it. Writing a date might be a useful thing to add when making your list. Nine items on that list had manifested, one I no longer needed or wanted, and one I still wanted. Having it, however, depended on the willingness of someone else to grant it. So I put away my list again, with a date added to that one item still missing. Another year passed, and I thought of that thing I wanted. To my surprise, the "wanting" energy was no longer there.

Having it or not, either way was just fine, and I felt deeply grateful for everything that had manifested.

I had reached a place of peace, where no longer wanting it would allow whatever outcome. Within a few weeks, the proposal to grant my wish was officially extended. Now the choice of accepting it or not was mine.

Sometimes our desires take a long time to manifest. Many years ago, it seemed impossible for me to return to Africa because it was not the policy of the firm to have expatriate women in Nigeria. Even wives stayed only for a limited time every year, and as for unmarried women–forget it! A flat *NO*. I needed a job so I took it anyway. I often went to the port to watch cargo ships leaving for Africa, while remembering the adventures of my first trip out there. It took two years, and then they offered me a job in Lagos as personal assistant to the CEO.

Problems will always arise in some form, but instead of pushing against them, let each situation be an opportunity to remind you of all the *other* things that are going well. From that higher vibration, you gain a higher perspective of a scary or unwanted situation.

Similarly, when I looked from a higher physical perspective at the havoc being wreaked by the Russian army in the town square, I was much less scared, in fact even interested in what went on down below than I had been earlier that morning, when on the same physical level as the soldiers. This holds true for your mental and emotional issues; they are really scary when you are on the level of the problem. Yet if you rise above it to identifying with Spirit and creating that gap between you and the situation, it will make all the difference.

THE POWER OF MANIFESTATION: GETTING WHAT YOU REALLY WANT

Circulate What You Want

Once you clearly see you are first and foremost a spiritual being, you also know you have all its attributes in potential and can activate them to flow into you.

However, if you keep your gifts and talents locked in without sharing them, they will stagnate and become lifeless just like a pond without an outlet. As you continue to give, share, and radiate, your talents and abilities will grow greater.

Receiving and giving is just like breathing. You cannot breathe in all the time or you'll explode; you cannot breathe out all the time or you'll pass out. First, you need to fill yourself up with what you want and need from your Source. When you feel complete and abundant, you have to find ways to give to the world what you feel you have in order to create more flow and more circulation, without which stagnation occurs. Find ways to activate more, even of what you think you don't have, so as to develop new talents and abilities, and then give even more to the world.

When you really get it, understand it's all within you, and that you can generate all the joy, fulfillment, and harmony of Source, the only question remaining is how to turn those qualities into the material things you desire. The very first thing to realize is that if it's already in you, all you have to do is let it out, so as to be in alignment with the Law of Circulation. And there is an arc to this law, which goes like this:

- ❖ We cannot give what we don't have, so must activate the feeling of "having" within.
- ❖ We cannot keep what we don't give, so we must give to ourselves and to others.
- ❖ We cannot sustain what we don't receive, so we must receive with gratitude what is extended to us.

And that's a very different thing from getting, or grabbing, from outside of us.

The Gifts of Giving

The best-selling author Derek Rydall encapsulated this principle into an exercise he named "The 7 Sacred Gifts,"[1] that are:
1. Giving forth,
2. Giving away,
3. Giving up,
4. Giving in,
5. Giving to yourself,
6. Giving thanks,
7. Forgiving.

Even if those seem simple, and we've heard it all before, only practicing them with a deeper awareness of what they really mean will yield us the outcomes that we are looking for. Hearing and intellectually understanding is one thing, but actually practicing it as a way of life and spiritually understanding it is quite another. Now that you know the bare bones of it, let's see what each of them really means.

Giving Forth: It does not necessarily mean giving money, although of course it can. But it also means giving freely of yourself, your time, your talents, and your abilities just for the joy of it. Giving forth is being of service in the world and supporting any venture that resonates with you, whether it's helping out in animal shelters, looking after destitute or handicapped children, or whatever is a service to anyone needing help or protection.

It means expressing your gifts to enliven and uplift others without expecting anything in return. I once saw a poet who was just reciting his poetry in the street, and people stopped to listen before they moved on, until, when he had finished, someone asked, "Where is your hat? That was beautiful!" He replied, "I can't afford to publish my poetry, and this way everyone can enjoy it." I remember I used to go out on a mountain trail just to be outside playing the guitar, and passing hikers were surprised there was no hat. All too often, we wait to be remunerated, or for something or someone to change, before we express our gift, blocking our expansion to the next level.

In order to bring in more financial abundance, you have to start by giving money. It doesn't matter how little, but give with the consciousness that you have something to give. There is a passage in the Bible where a rich man ostentatiously gave much money to the temple, while a poor old woman only gave a small coin, and Jesus said to his disciples, "Truly I say to you, this poor widow put in more than all the contributors to the treasury." (Mark 12:43) So it's all about a state of consciousness; the more you give from the place of being the Source of infinite wealth and abundance, the more you will have to give.

Giving Away: That's self-evident; you give away everything you don't need, don't use, and everything that's cluttering your drawers, your closet, your garage. The usual excuse is "I might need it some day!" or "When I lose weight, I'll wear it again." You do not trust the Universe to bring what you need, when you can see the abundance of nature everywhere around you.

As there is a circulation of breath, there is also a circulation of all things. So what you no longer use can be a Godsend to someone else, and, in addition, it creates a space for new things to flow to you, so you can grow to your next level.

Giving Up: Here, you start giving up old habits you don't even like having such as judging, criticizing, gossiping, and complaining. These are no longer congruent with the bigger vision or better version of yourself that you want to be; they're no longer congruent with your prayers and affirmations. You pray and affirm you're abundant, that you have the perfect partner, the ideal job, that the world is at peace–and then you negate or invalidate your affirmations through conversations about how bad the economy is, the latest terrorist attacks, or how mean and unfeeling your boss is.

Start having conversations about how much good you see in life, how people are helping in disaster areas, how refugees are being welcomed in their host countries, how schools are being built in remote parts of the world, and how trees are being planted in areas suffering from deforestation. In this way you will be giving birth to a new habit, one that is in alignment with your vision. You will have created a space in which what you have been asking for and praying for can manifest in your life.

Giving In: This means surrendering to the divine all your ideas about how your life is and how you want it change, whether it's in your job, or the people you're surrounded by. Surrender resisting what's trying to emerge through you. Surrender your prayers and intentions to have more and be more. Release all of it, the good and the bad, your need for things to look a certain way, your need for them to manifest at a certain time or with certain people. Do not hold on to any of it, but just surrender to the will of the divine to manifest your emergence into your next level in the way it wants it to be. Only then what is really trying to emerge, and not your idea of it, will manifest.

Giving to Yourself: This is a difficult one for most people, because from childhood, we have been taught not to be selfish, not to put ourselves forward, and to think of others first. We all are waiting for approval or validation from family, friends, or colleagues at work. But even when it's given, we can only accept it after we have given it to ourselves first. That is the meaning of self-love, because, once again, the Law of Circulation says you cannot sustain what you don't receive. So initially you have to fill yourself up with whatever you are trying to get from outside of you, and then from that place of fullness give it back out. Only then are you in a position to receive it.

Giving Thanks: Of course we know this. We've been taught to say "thank you" when we're given something, but do we really practice it to the fullest extent? Do we say "thank you" for all the things that appear in our life without our even asking? How much do we take for granted? Do we say "thank you" for the sun shining; for the life-giving rain; for the beauty of nature surrounding us; for the love of our pets; for having paved roads, electricity, indoor plumbing; or for schools, libraries, and museums with all the knowledge they contain? Do we say "thank you" for hospitals when we're ailing, right down to being grateful for having sight and hearing, which some people don't have?

There is a certain progression in the arc of gratitude:
1. First, we're grateful for nothing;
2. Then, we're grateful for something;
3. Then, we're grateful for everything;
4. And finally, we become grateful for no-thing again.

So we start in the victim mode and finally come full circle to just *being* grateful for no particular thing, no particular reason, and no-thing. We are simply living in a state of gratitude.

Forgiving: Just look at the word itself. You are focused on giving, not getting; you are "for" giving, not "for" getting. In fact, you are not withholding anything, including your love, respect, and appreciation, because you are willing to forget the perceived wrongdoing or hurt. When you can't forgive yourself or others, the energy of that is withholding. When someone owes you something, or you owe something, the energy of that is debt. And energetic debt often translates into actual financial debt. Basically, you're withholding–and remember that whatever's missing in your life is what you are not giving.

So when you are for-giving and willing to release others from their debt, and not withholding from anyone (or yourself!), you are also released from your debts. The Lord's Prayer is an invitation to do just that: "And forgive us our trespasses, as we forgive them that trespass against us." (Matthew 6:9–13) Then the floodgates of abundance can open. When you truly know you already have everything because of the Spirit dwelling in you, then you also recognize that no one could have taken anything away, nor added anything to you. You are whole and complete. So there never was anything to forgive–and that is the real and deep consciousness of forgiveness. When we have that consciousness, there cannot be blockages or lack of flow manifesting as financial debt. That is powerful!

Commitment is the Key to Success

Make it a commitment to focus on one or more of these gifts every day; or you can take a week to practice one, whichever feels good, then move on to the next one. If you practice this consistently, every day for a month, this way of thinking and acting will become a habit, and at the end you will not be the same person who started out. If you want something different in your life, you must first do something different. Then you become someone with a new perspective on the true nature of abundance, and of how life works.

The energy of giving and receiving is one circle; you cannot give unless you receive, and you cannot receive if you have not given. It's the Law of Circulation in action. When you don't act in accordance with a law, suffering results. The Bible verse "Cast your bread upon the waters; for thou shalt find it after many days" (Ecclesiastes 11:1) means the same thing. Only what you give out can return to you; it has your energetic signature. If things like anger, dishonesty, or abuse seem to be directed at you, examine when you have been those things in the past, if not to others, then to yourself. Have you always been completely honest and kind and loving to yourself? And if that's the case, which is unlikely, remember Spirit has chosen you to be its representative in the world. So meet those unwanted expressions that people seem to direct at you with understanding and compassion, knowing that if you had their challenges, their childhood, or if you were in their shoes, you would probably be acting that way, too.

You are the conduit through which the invisible qualities of Spirit become visible things, so you have to start giving. When you share your knowledge, do you have less of it at the end, or actually more? When you give of your music or art, do you finish with less at the end of a concert–even if it's for free–or more? Conversely, if you don't give–teach, paint, or sing–you will have fewer and fewer of those abilities.

The most effective way of getting what you want is by giving what you want to get. If you want more money, start giving what you can, but with the consciousness of having it to give. If you want more of a particular talent, give of that talent to others, even if it means singing to your cat or dancing with your dog. Don't wait until you get something in return, or you will be waiting forever. Start practicing and doing what you most want to do in the evenings or early mornings, on weekends, or whenever you find an hour or two. Whatever you practice you will improve, which brings its first rewards as you become a fulfilled and happy person.

Help Others Get What You Want

> *Your life is not about you. It has nothing to do with you. It has to do with everyone whose lives you touch, and the way in which you touch them.*
> —Neale Donald Walsch

When you decide to live not only for yourself and your immediate family, but for assisting others in whatever way to see their own potential–to express it, to become the best version of themselves–you will be living a life of service. That's the ingredient usually missing when you're depressed, unhappy, and think life is against you–service to others. Being centered just on yourself and feeling like a victim makes you constricted. When you expand to include others, you can forget, just for a moment, your own problems and misadventures. The less time you spend rehashing those, the happier your life can become. How you think and what you get eventually always matches.

If you want peace, joy, happiness, or confidence, find the places lacking it and give it there. Help others who are in difficult familial circumstances, whose health is failing, who are alone, who lack food, money, or just a friendly smile and a compassionate ear. You will sustain what you have and gradually gain more and more. The consciousness of helping others with whatever you have is the motor that brings more of those things into your own life. When a teacher helps students gain knowledge, the teacher finds they have more knowledge. The saying "You teach what you most need to learn" is very true; you get more insights, new perspectives on the subject, and the feedback you receive opens up more possibilities.

If you want more joy in your life, search out a place where you can give some joy. Visit a children's hospital with paper and a box of crayons and draw funny pictures to illustrate the stories you're telling. Giving them small silk pictures to paint that you will frame for them is wonderful. Dress up as a clown and make them laugh.

I know a harpist who takes her instrument to old people's homes, hospitals, even psychiatric institutions, and plays in the wards. The patients quiet down, become less aggressive, even fall asleep.

Visit an old people's home and just listen to the stories they have to tell about their lives that no one wants to hear. Make it a weekly visit, so they get to know you and have something to look forward to. I know of a lady who visits advanced-stage Alzheimer patients and quietly sings church hymns to them, holding their hands and with love in her heart. She seems one of the happiest people I ever saw, not to mention the happiness of the patients when someone is so totally with them.

If you want more connection with your own soul, more understanding of spiritual values, give what you already have to those who ask. Don't push, don't force or impose, but give when you see they want to hear more. Live your life according to your principles and share the understanding and knowledge you have. As the highest reality and most elevated expression of Spirit on this planet, you are a dispenser of divine gifts, which is your function in the world. The ancient Sanskrit word for man or human means "dispenser of divine gifts."

You must have noticed by now, that as you achieve a desire, another one comes up. You have learned how to manifest what you want, but is that really enough for you? Maybe you're realizing that nothing material will ever truly fulfill you. So you will want to explore how to get to the next level where only the most courageous ones dare to go. We will be exploring that in chapter 6, but for now let's look at why so often things seem to fall apart before falling together again.

Why Things Get Worse before Getting Better

Problems will always arise in some form, even when, and often because, you have activated a higher vision. Now that you've designed a life to mobilize the qualities underlying your desires, you feel problems shouldn't arise. But suddenly you're feeling scared, sad, or depressed, and things seem to be breaking down, falling apart, and not working. What's really happening is that you've brought to the surface deeper unconscious patterns, everything that is unlike your new, higher vision for your life. They were hidden until your vision brought them up to be dissolved.

Through all the practices you have just learned–the shadow work, values conflicts, living in the feeling-tone–you have been able to observe and release. The Truth is that you are a pure, undistorted, and all-powerful expression of Spirit, able to dissolve everything unlike itself. Realize that those feelings do not stop you, but rather they serve to make you stronger and more determined to fulfill your vision. Do whatever needs to be done in the moment; then bring your attention back to the highest perspective and true beliefs.

Beliefs Dictate Experiences

Your old beliefs are still there, active until you change them, and they color your perception. We don't see reality; we only see our perception of reality. An extreme example of this is the story of the invisible Spanish ships when Columbus reached the New World. It has been said that his crew came ashore in small rowboats, having anchored the large ships farther out; however, the natives could not see those ships at first. In their frame of reference, they knew all about small craft, but anything as large as those ships was beyond their comprehension. Only their shaman, who noticed something was blocking the waves at one spot, eventually perceived one ship and then the others. He was able to impart his viewpoint to the rest of his tribe, who then saw the ships, too.

The belief active in your consciousness will influence the experiences you have. I have had burglars in my house twice in my twenty-seven years of living in Africa; being burgled was not in my consciousness. To some, this was a regular occurrence every year or so.

How can you change your beliefs so they align with your desires? Start questioning them. See whether they are still true for you now. Most of them are not even yours, but have been imposed on you by parents, teachers, and society, or are collective beliefs held for centuries.

There are countless examples of this: The belief established at age four that you have to hold your mother's hand when crossing a street. The belief that only good and patriotic people are put in prison–that's one I held for years! The belief that the earth is flat,

THE POWER OF MANIFESTATION: GETTING WHAT YOU REALLY WANT

that it's impossible to run a mile in less than four minutes, or that the human body cannot withstand moving at a speed over thirty to forty miles an hour without breaking down in some way.

Sometimes, it's simply more practical to act according to a false belief. When we build a doghouse in the back yard, we draw the plans as if the earth were flat. It's easier, more convenient, and on the scale of a doghouse, makes no difference. But we don't actually believe the earth is flat: we still know the truth.

Every belief will act as a law *for you* until you change it, either because you have had direct experience that negates it, or you have replaced it with another one that is more congruent with the person you have evolved into now. You may accept a new viewpoint from someone you trust. Unless a belief is an expression of absolute truth, such as there is only harmony, peace, love, abundance, and goodness everywhere, everything else is relative, subject to change, and just a belief, not a truth.

> Unless a belief is an expression of absolute truth, such as there is only harmony, peace, love, abundance, and goodness everywhere, everything else is relative, subject to change, and just a belief, not a truth.

Believe in the Absolute, Not the Relative Truth

Absolute truth pertains to your spiritual being and will permeate your physical being if you allow it. A relative truth pertains to the material world and is always subject to change. The inherent perfection of absolute truth can never be altered by your perception of it. It simply always is. But your perception will dictate your experience.

Just as when you take a picture of a landscape, the picture shows only a part of the whole landscape you have seen. It shows the camera's perception, where the colors may be a little different from what you remember. There may be distortions or other imperfections depending on how clean or perfect the lens of the camera is. But the picture is only a representation of what you've seen, and makes you remember what the landscape was like. The more you look at it, the more you think the real landscape was like the picture you see, which is not the truth, since there was a filter on your lens, a crack, or a smudge. Yet you never think your picture is the real landscape, or that the real landscape will be affected if you spill your coffee on the photo or it gets torn. So looking at the visible expression of life, you are just looking at the picture of ultimate perfection, not at the Truth.

In the same way, the absolute truth of perfect harmony, joy, peace, love, and abundance of every good thing cannot be affected by the choices you make or the perceptions you have as a human being. The only things that will be affected are the experiences you have in your life. The more aligned you are with the real landscape, the absolute perfection existing everywhere, the better your material life will become.

Whatever the situation you're facing, remember your potential is always greater than the problem. From times immemorial we have been told, "And ye shall know the truth, and the truth shall make you free." (John 8:33) Practice knowing the truth in the face of all appearances that seem to deny it, and it must manifest.

THE POWER OF MANIFESTATION: GETTING WHAT YOU REALLY WANT

EXERCISE

Look at any issue you have right now, any threshold in your way, and first, talk yourself back to all the spiritual truths you know: *"God is all there is; being infinite, omnipotent and omnipresent, there can't be a life other than God or a power other than God. So there can't be God and anything else. And if there can't be God and anything else, right where I am must be all of God. So where I am must be the wholeness and perfection of God, because there is not 'God and me' there is only 'God as me.'"* Keep reminding yourself of all the Truths you know and can remember until you start feeling they are really true.

When you get to the resonance with your true Self that you have just activated and feel, *This is the truth about me! I am that Spirit inside me!* you'll notice some of the anxiety leaving you. You'll have a little more peace, more trust that everything will turn out all right. And the next thing to do is rest in that awareness of peace, not letting in any doubt, despondency, fear, or disbelief.

This is not a practice you do once, and it's finished. You practice it over and over, every time you sense the fear or doubt come up again. Because it will! It needs your determined effort and consistency to give you the results you want. Every time the issue reappears, stop. Don't resist or fight it; become still, get back to the truth of who you know you are, and turn the outcome over to God. And every time you do that and surrender, resting in that feeling of connection to your Spirit, a little piece of the ego that wants to fight and defend itself is dissolved, and more of your spiritual self becomes apparent.

Working in this way is building structures that will uphold the truth of your being. That truth is evident everywhere around you in nature. Abundance, beauty, harmony, joy in the birds that sing, the thousands of leaves on every tree, the way seasons follow each other, or night follows day; even if sometimes days are longer, or shorter, it all balances out at the end of the year. But unless you can connect with that universal law of goodness and perfection, it doesn't do you any good. You have to know it first, and then live in alignment with it; just as electricity, which is everywhere, doesn't light your house or cook your meal unless you have the structures that harness it, making it useful. Through consistent practices you build the structures for the perfection of the spiritual life to appear in the visible world.

Look at Appearances, but See Perfection

There is a difference between looking and seeing. While we look at the world as it is, as it appears, we can see what we choose to see: a disaster, or an opportunity for compassion to be sent out energetically. Looking at a diseased body, we can see the perfection of the Spirit inhabiting that body. Looking at terrorists, we can have compassion for their sense of separation from the divine–or they simply could not be committing such atrocities. That's not condoning criminal activities. We must do all in our power to stop them, but never lose sight of the fact that even criminals have the same Spirit within them we have, and so need more love and compassion, not less. But we also stop destructive activities if we can, or physically remove ourselves from their vicinity, while energetically sending out blessings.

THE POWER OF MANIFESTATION: GETTING WHAT YOU REALLY WANT

Your soul is always trying to express more of itself through you, and your issue is an indication of where you are not in alignment, and where you have not activated some qualities needed for your continued evolution. You simply don't know what those qualities are, or you would have activated them long ago. Now is the time to ask some questions to help you discover them. Once you recognize these qualities, all you have to do is consciously cultivate them in every area of your life.

EXERCISE

First ask:

A. *If this situation was never to change, if this problem was never to go away, if this issue was to be permanent, what qualities would I need to express, who would I have to become to be truly joyful and free even in the midst of this? How to still live a fulfilled and productive life?*

    You might discover that if you could have a greater sense of peace or greater trust, the situation would not bother you as much. Or you'd have to become more patient, more forgiving, more harmonious, selfless, expansive, discerning, considerate. . . . Just be with each feeling in turn; let the necessary qualities come up, and write out that list, whatever it is for you.

B. *And then envision being on the other side of the situation. Imagine that it was resolved, gone, or healed: what would be your feelings now? What would you be expressing? What would be the qualities of your being?*

Joy and gratitude, of course! Showing you that you always need to consciously exercise those. But what else? Perhaps empowerment, generosity, or you would feel greater confidence, security, freedom, or clarity.

So now you have two lists of qualities, one for if this situation were never to change, the other for it being miraculously solved. You might have some of the same qualities in each list. Make a master list of all of them together, and those are the qualities you need to practice and cultivate now, regardless of your situation.

Your Vision Can Only Manifest through You

What you have just discovered is that the qualities you have written are the next stage of your evolution. That is the more expanded self, wanting to emerge; a self that is peaceful, confident, empowered and free. This situation is really a catalyst for you to evolve into that next stage of your being. And while the crisis feels like a bad thing, it's really an opportunity to become who and what you are really meant to be. But it requires a paradigm shift from just problem-solving. You must become a vision-holder.

By asking such empowering questions, you lift your frequency and embody a higher vibration than that of the problem and it can now dissolve. Just solving a problem is never the complete answer, because you have not raised your frequency, so another problem will soon appear. The only permanent solution is lifting your frequency out of the range of those problems. Really understand this: the distance between where you are and the life you want to live is not a distance in time and space. It's a distance in frequency.

The vision you have can only come to life through you becoming more of You–or you would have manifested it already. As Gandhi once said, "You must be the change you wish to see in the world."[2] Likewise you must become the change you want to see in your life. You must become congruent with the energy of your vision. Then your body or your affairs begin to reshape themselves around that higher frequency, and the world calls it a healing, or a lucky break, while you know that more of you just emerged.

If you're feeling stuck, it's because you have rules for what your success should look like and what you let yourself think or believe. You don't look outside the box of what you're used to, of things that have always worked in the past.

Think of a fly trying to get out of a room. It spent all summer flying in and out of that window–it got used to it. Now that winter is coming, you open your window for just a little while, then close it again. The fly took that moment to fly in, get comfortable and warm. But when it wanted out again, flying towards the trees and sky out there, it bumped against the glass. It kept trying and trying and every time got a hard knock on the head. Even if you open the window for the fly, it doesn't think of going around the edge to fly out, rather it keeps bumping into the same place from where it can see the sky. It doesn't think there is another way around the side of the window.

Don't be like that fly.

To get unstuck, you have to open up to a new kind of thinking. So change your personal rules for success; search out new behaviors and attitudes. Break out of your routines, even those that have worked in the past. We have now moved into a new paradigm, where old rules often don't apply. We have to think new thoughts, leading to different actions and untried ways of doing things. Be willing to be a little uncomfortable for a while, for the sake of growth. Then you get familiar with the new dimension and enjoy it, but soon start searching for an even greater dimension–forever, because change is the only constant in the world of form.

Whatever is happening right now, whatever it looks like, remember it's just an appearance. So don't get scared and stop your practice. Those appearances must and will change as you consistently keep doing the work and bringing your attention back to who you really are. Those unconscious beliefs now surfacing about things not working, and feelings of not being good enough or clever enough, are lower vibrations, no longer congruent with the higher vision you've activated. It's natural. They must come to the surface to be flushed out of your system or transmuted. It's a part of your growth, your healing, and your transformation. And in order to become more, you must transform. Lose or abandon some things, activate others. Any negativity surfacing is a sign you're making progress, and if you just keep going, keep shining your highest Light, these thoughts and feelings cannot stop you. On the contrary, they will propel you forward even more powerfully. Now you're really ready for a new, more expanded life–and this is just the beginning of the next step in your evolution.

Review of chapter 5:
- ❖ Solving a problem lies in lifting your awareness out of the frequency of the problem and into the frequency of Source.
- ❖ There is a deeper purpose to your life than just material achievements. Find your highest vision and live it.
- ❖ Your current situation is only the result of your thoughts of yesterday.
- ❖ Spirit answers your every prayer instantly, but you can only experience it when your frequency is close to that of Spirit.
- ❖ Giving out, circulating what you have, is the only way to receive more.

CHAPTER 6

THE POWER OF SURRENDER: RELEASING ALL RESISTANCE

One morning, like countless times before, my husband was leaving for the Lomé airport. An hour later, I was surprised to see him walk in again: "The flight has been delayed, and I can't stay long, just wanted to say good-bye again. I love you so much!" This had never happened, even though flights were routinely delayed. I felt a very special quality about his hug, even if I did not fully recognize the gift I had received until a few hours later, when two policemen came in to say the plane had crashed into the swamps on take-off. The only survivor was my husband, in a coma.

The police were guarding the intensive care unit, and I was not allowed in to see him. My only prayer was to have him come back, have him live. Two days later Marc died without recovering consciousness. If breaking the news of the accident to my thirteen-year-old son had been hard, telling him this was the end was even harder. I felt shattered, but had to stay strong. No child should see the only parent they have left totally fall apart.

Now came urgent practical considerations: I had to leave a life of over twenty-seven years in Africa within a month—the work permit was Marc's. I had no money—the bank account was in his name. There were legal issues since the causes of the crash were unclear. Swiss Embassy issues. Police issues. Packing up the house issues. Deciding where to go: England, where

I had my family, or Switzerland, because I was Swiss, or the States, where my brother lived. Funeral arrangements and shipping the coffin problems. The list went on and on, and I felt as if I was moving knee-deep through sand. Every step a huge effort, not really resolving anything, just leading to more difficulties.

A couple of days before my flight out, I looked around at my half-empty house, thought of all the unresolved issues, and knew it was impossible to get all of that done in the time left. Totally impossible. I was also mentally, emotionally, and physically exhausted. I remember I sat down with the thought I give up all struggle and trying to get things done. Things will be what they will be and that's OK. *I fully accepted any outcome, didn't want to know what it would be, and relinquished all control, totally surrendered. A feeling of peace, a release of tension flooded over me, and I relaxed for the first time in a month. In this moment, I needed nothing, wanted nothing, had nothing, and was empty and totally peaceful. It brought back the image of me at twelve years old, sitting in a strange military barracks in total despair, and then having this feeling of needing nothing, wanting nothing. It was the same peace with no apparent cause, the same feeling of relief brought up through total surrender.*

My prayers did not get answered: I had lost my husband; had to leave Africa and a life I loved; had to raise my son alone in a country I didn't know; had to get a job in a highly technological setting when I had never even had an electric typewriter. It seemed like everything was against me. But because of my letting go and letting God, I was now at peace. And the ultimate result of not getting the only thing I wanted was a much more expanded and different life than I could have possibly imagined. At that time, I did not know I would have to experience more despair and an even bigger loss before I was ready and able to live my soul's purpose.

THE POWER OF SURRENDER: RELEASING ALL RESISTANCE

What Surrendering Is–and What It Is Not

All you have discovered so far has allowed you to develop a sense that everything you want and need is already within you, that there is a higher vision and deeper purpose to life than what you've thought. You realized that all your challenges and problems are only there to help you grow and become more of who you really are, and that everything is working for your ultimate good. Having uncovered a bigger vision for your life, you are now willing to live it with a feeling of empowerment and having more control. You know where you want to go and how to get there. So now I have good news, and bad news! The bad news is that you have to let go of control, just when you've really mastered it. And the good news is that it will ultimately give you more power, because Spirit is pushing you forward into a life you cannot imagine right now. That's the secret power of surrender.

There is always a next stage of growth, and now your soul's idea for your life is trying to unfold. If you're still struggling, it's probably because you are holding on to an old idea of who you are, or what your life should look like. If you want to get to the next level, let go of everything you have learned. You can only take yourself so far as a human, and the next stage is mastering the art of surrendering to a higher, spiritual order.

That doesn't mean giving in to circumstances, but on the contrary, opening up to your guidance and allowing more of You out. It means yielding to a greater potential, a larger life, and a more powerful, divine energy. In the words of Derek Rydall, "An acorn surrenders to the oak tree that's trying to emerge; it doesn't acquiesce to the broken shell."[1] I've had to surrender many times, and I know how hard it can be, especially when things are sudden, really painful, and confusing.

You can only attain so much with mental and emotional exercises. If you gained control of your life through the work we've done together, but are still feeling stuck in some area, you now have to surrender to a higher order. This is not the time to try harder, to work even more; it's time to let go of control and surrender to the unknown, the divine ideas that are revealed only one step at a time. You will not necessarily see the ultimate destination, which may be very different from what you first envisaged, but even grander than your best idea.

Release Attachment to Outcomes

When we think of surrendering, we usually start by letting go of the how, when, and where, but still hold on to the what. I want a job, a partner, or a house. We have surrendered the idea that the job has to pay at least xyz. We have surrendered the idea that the partner must look or be a certain way, or that the house must be in this or that neighborhood. This is not total surrender. Total surrender means we let go of the idea of even having a job, a partner, or a house. If it means living on the street, that's OK. If it means we stay alone, that's OK too–our own company and that of the Spirit within is enough.

> A surrendered intention and action means letting go of any attachment to the outcome.

But it doesn't mean we let go of all desires, or intentions. It doesn't mean we stop doing things. We still have intentions, we still take actions because we are a living, breathing expression of the Divine; but a surrendered intention and action means letting go of any attachment to the outcome. When you truly see Spirit

THE POWER OF SURRENDER: RELEASING ALL RESISTANCE

is the animating principle, the Consciousness of the physical self, then any action you take must originate from Spirit and be for the highest good.

Main Stages of Human Consciousness

There are four main stages of human consciousness: victim, victor, vehicle, and unity. They are all very necessary for our development, just as every stage of physical growth is necessary to reach the next one. You start as a baby, grow into a child, a teenager, a young adult, and a mature person. That is a linear progression; once past a stage, you never revert to being a child or a baby again. Where consciousness is concerned, the stages are not linear; you can go back and forth between them, depending on circumstances. But just for the sake of clarity, let's consider them in a linear fashion and also stay aware that in each stage you have to let go of something to get to the next stage.

You already understand that ultimately there is only one power, and, because of oneness, you are at the point of that power. Your growth into the full realization of who you are looks like this:

Victim mode. First, even though you are at the point of power, you are not aware of it and therefore feel like a victim of circumstances. In order to access that power, you have to take full responsibility for your life, see what you really want, and move out of victimhood into the next stage of your evolution, the victor consciousness. You must become fully conscious of where you are and what you feel, so nothing unconscious can run your life; then take action towards implementing your vision. You start creating your reality.

Victor mode. Here, you are motivated by the desires of your personal will: what you want, what you need, what you wish to achieve. And your consciousness tells you that even if you've created all those wonderful things, you have also created all your pain and suffering, and you simply don't know how to solve that. You tell yourself, "Look at all you've achieved; you should be happy," but you're not. That's because you have been creating from a place of feeling separate from Source. It prepares you for a more spiritual understanding, where you come to realize a deeper purpose to life than just getting material possessions and a deeper reason for why certain unwanted situations manifest. Slowly, you go beyond the personal will to cultivate a higher understanding, but it still requires your personal will to maintain that awareness, to remember to live in it. As you do that, you start creating from the heart, which also includes the mind; you create from Unity with Spirit.

Vehicle mode. The next stage of your evolution is to realize you are not really creating anything. You're just an avenue through which all the aspects of the divine can flow–in accordance with the choices you make through free will. It's the vehicle consciousness, and it has a lot to do with faith and trust in the divine. It's a consciousness that says, "Everything that happens in my world, every adversity, every conflict that's facing me, every negative thought and feeling I have, can only be catalysts from the divine Spirit to facilitate the healing and transformation of those parts of me that still need it, and to help me reach my next highest level of evolution." This consciousness has you constantly searching how to meet the painful or unwanted situation from a higher consciousness than you had in both victim and victor consciousness.

Unity consciousness. To advance from being a conduit to unity consciousness, you have to let go of the personal sense of self and become unity, a state of oneness with all things. In order to progress, in each stage you have to let go of something. To go from victim to victor, you let go of victimhood; to go from victor to vehicle, you let go of control; and to go from vehicle to Unity, you let go of the personal sense of self. Again, these stages are not linear, and we tend to go in and out of the first three, depending on events and circumstances.

THE POWER OF SURRENDER: RELEASING ALL RESISTANCE

Change Your Meaning for Events

As you go through your day, it's a matter of having faith in everything being the absolute perfection of divinity and surrendering all the ideas you collected up to now. No matter how you feel about a situation, about life, or about what's happening, you trust that this is just another catalyst for your evolution. You don't have to like it, or see some special "spiritual" meaning in it. Give yourself permission to resent it, to hate it, to be angry or revolted: it's still for your further evolution. And you might find that by acknowledging those "negative" feelings as part of you and fully feeling them, they tend to dissolve. Accepting them is unnecessary; they are there, whether you accept them or not. Acknowledge them as expressions of energy through you without judgment; you are the director of how that energy is to express. If it's through anger, so be it! Pound your pillows, but don't take it out on other people. Love it as just energy, and you will find it transmutes itself.

If your life seems to be non-stop problems, collisions, and bumps, it's only doing it so you can come out at the other end perfectly polished and beautiful like the gems that are put through a stone polishing machine.

So far, you have been changing the thoughts, feelings, and patterns in your mind. All of that was necessary and still has a place in the future, but now you can add changing what things mean for you. Instead of an event symbolizing adversity or being a block, you take it as proof of your higher alignment with Spirit. Rather than things needing to be fixed or changed, you are changing your perspective. You understand you are going through a transformation now, instead of thinking it's somewhere up ahead once you have acted differently.

In vehicle consciousness, you have faith in everything being the perfection of Source–but the challenge is in how the world gives you all kinds of proof there is something other than the divine and that people continue to act in ways that are not divine. Therefore, it's up to you to be rooted in your own heart, in the knowing and acceptance that everything is the highest will of Spirit, even the things you think are inappropriate or evil. You perceive there is a divine purpose to everything. You don't have to know what it is; you just know it must be so. For as long as it takes, keep reaffirming that to yourself, in the face of not feeling it and it not appearing in your world. Let me repeat that: *As long as it takes!* Never give up. This energy that you cultivate in silence, within yourself, will radiate out into the world, causing it to shift and change and ultimately reflect back to you the energy you have put out. When your internal spiritual alignment is peaceful and harmonious, more than blaming and vengeful, the outside world will, over time, reflect that back to you.

The human perception of reality is material and false; surrendering it will align you with spiritual Reality. So long as you believe the false perception, you live under the laws of duality, of good/bad, illness/health. When you believe Truth, you live under the laws of unity, wholeness, and goodness. For you, duality no longer exists, and "bad" no longer exists.

Letting go of your misperceptions will automatically place you in a higher reality; just as when you're driving along a desert road and it looks like there's water over it. But you know there's no water there. It's just a mirage. So you don't stop the car and wait for it to dry. You don't even have to pray for the water to go away; you *know* it's not there. You still see the appearance of it, but you know it's not real, so you keep driving. Often, misperceptions stop you from doing what you really want because you think you're not good enough, not educated enough, don't have the money, the know-how, or you're too young or too old. You forget the Spirit that dwells within you is omniscient and omnipotent, and consequently don't go for your dream. Instead, stand tall and do what it takes again and again to actually make it work–while surrendering the outcome of your efforts.

THE POWER OF SURRENDER: RELEASING ALL RESISTANCE

Various Levels of Surrender

There are various kinds of surrender. There is partial surrender when you say, "I don't know . . . ," and surrender the *how* and the *when* but keep the *what*, the outcome, still in mind. There is the "I give up" mindset, which is not surrender to a higher order, but a response to material pain and suffering without invoking the divinity within.

There is also the scenario where you have done everything you could humanly do, nothing is working out, even time is running out, and you end up turning it all over to divinity, totally accepting whatever will be the outcome.

Then there is the highest form of surrender, where you say, "I don't know how to do this, so I hand over all control to divinity–which I AM–to do through me and for me what I, of my own self, cannot do." You listen to guidance and keep making the highest choices without any attachment to the outcome. That's surrendered action.

In my story of leaving Africa, I had to surrender. Nothing was being accomplished in the legal, banking, or the logistics areas, for it was all outside my control. I had spent almost a month on all of it, and now it simply could not be done. I sat in the middle of the room and thought of God giving me impossible tasks and said to Him, "Unless you do it, it won't get done and that's OK! The ball is in your court!" I truly gave up all thought, all control, all preferences to the divine; outcomes did not exist for me in that moment. The relief I felt was huge.

That same afternoon, two couples of neighbors showed up saying, "We thought you could use some help with packing up the house!" Later, the bank manager arrived with a sheaf of papers to sign and a briefcase full of cash, and he was accompanied by the police commissioner who stayed with me for two days, then took me to the airport and even into the plane. The consul from the embassy came with permits for whatever, and the lawyer with more papers to sign. A friend arrived to take my son to the movies and dinner. The house was full of people and everything was being done without my having to go anywhere or do anything. That is the power of total surrender. But if nothing had been resolved in those last two days, my feelings would have been exactly the same. Relief and peace.

The fully conscious way is where you choose to surrender first, because you know that what appears is for your ultimate good. You surrender *before* you have exhausted all the material ways of dealing with your issue, and only go to the physical avenues available when in that state of having turned it over to Spirit first. It's a little more difficult, but absolutely radical. As a vehicle, you are not trying to do God's job, but acknowledging God's perfection and allowing the Universe to do everything through you. Once you fully and consciously surrender, the will of God becomes your own.

> Life does not have to be convenient to be perfect: convenience is rooted in duality, but perfection is unity.

When you attempt to manifest a different reality than what is, you are taking control. When you say you want to co-create your own reality, you are unknowingly refusing to surrender to Spirit's ideas. But as a vehicle for Spirit, you know everything is perfect; it may not be perfect in the way you want it to be, but it's perfect as the quickest way for your highest evolution.

Most times, we confuse perfection with convenience. When you contemplate the highest idea of perfection for your life, it boils down to what is most convenient. Life does not have to be convenient to be perfect: convenience is rooted in duality, but perfection is unity. When you don't need to have things being or looking a certain way, you are truly heart-centered and flexible. You are open to experiencing what appears without judging it, or yourself, as lacking or less-than. You know the perfection of Source permeates everything, you included. So you must be in spiritual alignment, whether it's convenient for the personality, or not.

Letting Go of Control Is Surrender

It's counterintuitive to let go of control now that you have achieved and manifested so much with the exercises and processes outlined in chapters 4 and 5, but it's absolutely necessary if you want to get to the next level. People who have achieved great things, even miracles, have had to go beyond victor consciousness to become the vehicle through which could manifest the higher powers of the Spirit they knew they were.

Surrendering does not mean you give up desiring or wanting to achieve things, and not do much. On the contrary, the more surrendered you are, the busier you become. But there is a difference between desiring something and wanting something. The word *desire* comes from the root "of the sire" or "Spirit": Spirit's every quality is already in you, in a dormant state, which you have to awaken and let out. You can trust your desire because it gives you clues as to what's trying to emerge. Surrendering means commitment to doing whatever it takes to allow that desire to emerge, but you're not attached to what it must look like. You are in the world doing things, but not "of it."

And that doesn't mean just coasting along, going with the flow along a river. If you do that, you might get caught up among some dead wood and stopped, or reach a waterfall and go over the edge. You must have an intention, but you're not attached to the material outcome. You know that what's unfolding in your life might be coming through a filter of parental or cultural conditioning so that, really, you don't know what you want. You think you want more money or a bigger car, but it's really the qualities of wealth and abundance that you want. They may not necessarily manifest at first as dollars or cars; it may be friends, business partners, or a wealth of inspiration. Be willing to notice and appreciate all forms of your qualitative desire without attachment to the picture in your mind, the outcome.

Wanting something implies an absence of it, while a desire doesn't have an attachment to the outcome; it carries a vibration of "Wouldn't it be nice if . . . " When aligned with Source, you surrender your wants, but always say "yes" to your desires. And when things become hard, or don't work out the way you want them to, instead of going back into victim mode, lamenting and whining, you recognize that since this unwanted circumstance has appeared, it must be the quickest and most direct way for you to grow into what your soul already is.

Surrendering Is Consciously Recognizing a Higher, Spiritual Order for Things

In order to move from victor consciousness, where you're the co-creator of your reality, into the next stage of your evolution, which is being a conduit for the will of Spirit to manifest through you, it's necessary to surrender your own will, your own ideas as to how your life unfolds, and even what unfolds, without giving up, without being passive and just waiting for things to happen. On the surface, it seems impossible, especially when you've become so good at manifesting almost everything you want. How do you stay active, participate in and improve a life that sometimes gets painful and difficult, while at the same time surrendering?

What is causing your life to be painful is not the things that happen, but the reasons you think they happen, otherwise known as "your understanding." You're saying, "This happened because . . .; I'm angry because . . .," and you're blaming someone or something for the way you're feeling; however, it's your reasons about how life should be that are making you unhappy and resentful. Try living from the idea of "I don't know." Eliminate the word *because* and say, "I'm angry, but I don't know why I am angry." Immediately you feel unconcerned, more peaceful, and being angry even seems a little ridiculous, so you manage a laugh at yourself.

We resist the idea of not knowing, because our whole upbringing–school, college, and jobs–was focused on knowing. When you think you know, it creates a belief in right and wrong, and immediate conflict: I'm right, and you're wrong. Things in themselves are not right or wrong; they are only right or wrong *for you*. So rather than knowing, which creates conflict, let's open up to the idea of not knowing, which leaves you in a state of love and acceptance.

Living From a Place of Not Knowing

As soon as you honestly admit you don't know, Spirit can take over and start doing for you what you don't know how to do, or what you don't know how to stop doing. Spirit can only do things through you, so if you stay open to new ideas and different avenues that appear–and keep doing whatever seems best at the moment with the consciousness that you don't know but Spirit does–your attachment to the outcome dissolves. Whatever happens is OK. You don't have to like it or agree with it, and it may be upsetting or inconvenient for the personality. But you know that you are more than your personality; so you take refuge in "I don't know," which is so freeing and liberating in a moment of upset, while automatically raising your vibration. That's the energetic solution to any problem, and if you stay in that consciousness, it's only a matter of time before the material expression also changes.

When you're honest, you realize that your consciousness, or God, is with you *as* you, now and in every moment. You are the expression of divinity in physical form right now whatever you are doing. Spirit is all Love. It's up to you to make your every thought, feeling, and action in as perfect an alignment as possible with that Love.

Honesty leads you to love and self-love as Spirit. It's enough to accept yourself as you are, with all the parts of you that feel in pain, incapable, ugly, not good enough, because the only reason for them to sabotage you is that they've not been loved and accepted in the same way as all the beautiful, joyous, capable, and talented parts. Those parts are sad and in pain, so love them and hold them close, as you would hold a child who's just caught their hand in the door. You don't know when the pain will stop, but you will hold them in your arms and love them until it does. Do the same for all those rejected aspects that are clamoring for acceptance.

> Surrender the belief that you of your own self can do anything; then call on your higher truth to guide you.

This does not mean you abandon all knowing and understanding; but rather than searching for the reasons of a situation with your mind, admit you don't know and let the understanding naturally come from Spirit. You are not refusing to know and understand; you are just not in charge of it. That is surrendering to higher wisdom. It's being aligned with truth and honesty. It doesn't mean you don't participate in life. You still make choices and take action, but now you work in harmony with your true nature. Surrender the belief that you of your own self can do anything; then call on your higher truth to guide you.

When you have reasons why things happen, you get angry, sad, or upset. When you refuse to contemplate the reasons, you can be at peace. The next time you get cut off in traffic, try not to understand why it happened, and you will immediately be at peace. If you think you know–they're stupid, they're unconscious, they should have their license taken away, they nearly killed me!–now you're angry, upset, and likely to cause an accident yourself. But if you stay in the consciousness of "I don't know why this happened! It just did!" your feelings don't get stirred. You're peaceful.

If you think you know why your boss is yelling at you–you made a mistake, you didn't do your job, or you were late for work–now you are afraid, upset, or angry. If you stay in the consciousness of "I don't know why he's yelling–he must have a reason, but *I* don't have a reason"–your world is not shattered into a thousand pieces. Things are going to happen in your life. Your consciousness doesn't determine what happens. However, it does determine the quality of your experience: you're either going to have a peaceful and happy existence, or a not so peaceful one. When you admit you don't know, then you're no longer in control and have relinquished it to the part of you that knows everything.

Listening to Your Soul

Your mind is your ego talking. You need to listen to your soul whispering there is a higher, spiritual order for everything, which must be recognized by the human self even if you don't know what it is. Spirit is in charge of everything, but as it incarnated, it gave you free will to either align with its agenda, or choose differently. If what you want is not manifesting–or you don't like what's manifesting–recognize it's not against you, but an opportunity to discern that a higher wisdom than your own is in operation here, to further your evolution. Maybe the time was not right for what you wanted; maybe other things had to come into alignment first; or maybe you had to somehow change before the project could work.

I certainly did not want to lose my husband, yet it opened me up to spiritual values, which I resisted and would not have developed in a safe and comfortable environment. The challenges I faced then strengthened my independence and reliance on Spirit rather than on people. I had to change before I could attain a vehicle consciousness, and only hardships would do that. None of us willingly change while we have a comfortable life and no worries. So in order to grow, we need to be shaken out of our comfort zone.

Once you totally let go of control, a shift happens and you become the vehicle through which spirit expresses into the world. You are like the violin for the musician who expresses his talent through the instrument. It's not up to the instrument to tell the musician which piece to play, where to play it, or how to play it. In the same way, you know that, of your own self, you have no music, no power; the only music and power you have is breathed into you by your soul. Your role is to let your soul pour whatever it wants through you, knowing it can only give perfection, since that's what your soul is. Accept every appearance as a gift and trust it must be for your highest good, even if right now it looks like the worst thing you've ever had happen.

Don't even go into how, or why, unwanted or painful situations are for your highest evolution. Every situation comes from your Consciousness, so accept it as a gift, even if you don't like it. Don't confuse perfection with convenience. It was highly inconvenient for me to leave West Africa, which had become home after more than twenty-seven years, and inconvenient to start a new life bearing no resemblance to the one I knew, with no family and no support; however, it was the perfect gift for my evolution, even if I did not recognize it then. Whatever the event for you that's unwanted, disturbing, and inconvenient, acknowledge it as an expression of God's perfection regardless of how it appears. I did not see my challenges as gifts–it took many painful years and another traumatic experience to at last start seeing from a higher perspective.

Everything in the world of form–and that includes your thoughts and emotions–is an expression of the perfection of Spirit, even if it looks very imperfect to you. Try to see every situation as a perfect expression of whatever it is. That inconvenient event is a perfect example of inconvenience; the frustration you're feeling is a perfect example of frustration. This attitude will free you from judging circumstances and allow you to feel whatever you are feeling without judging yourself. You allow the Universe to act through you. When you endeavor to manifest a different reality, it's an attempt to take control. When you surrender, you acknowledge the situation and open to knowing there is a higher perspective from which to view it. Everything may not be perfect in the way you want it to be, but it's a perfect expression of whatever it is–now you have released judgment.

Abandon the idea that perfection is when things are the way you want them to be. Surrender wanting to have your own way, and you will end up having far more than you ever thought possible. The question of how to surrender and how to let go is an all-pervading one. It requires you to do something that you don't know how to do. So instead, first acknowledge that you don't know and ask Spirit to do through you and as you, what you don't know how to do. And keep taking inspired action.

"Ask and ye shall receive" (John 16:24) is a promise given us centuries ago.

We Can Have Material Good after Surrendering

Since your primary identification is with the physical body, you most desire physical things. Things are just expressions in density of the energy that is only love and perfection, and when you surrender to Spirit, you activate all it is spiritually to express as material things through your focused thoughts and actions.

Considering you also face problems that are the expressions of your past thoughts, you often speak in the negative: "I don't want to have this problem," or " I don't want to look for another job." Or you create positive affirmations: "I am abundant!" and "I am healthy!"

which you don't really believe because your reality shows you the opposite. In either case, your identification is with your material self and your frequency is that of lack and limitation. As soon as you switch your identification to your spiritual Self, you realize the Source of everything that is good and perfect cannot be poor, sick, or have any problem. So when you say, "I'm poor," or "I'm sick," you're stating an untruth in regard to who you really are. To put it another way, the Source of all that IS cannot "not be," so it doesn't recognize concepts such as no, not, don't, and cannot. When you say, "I don't want to be poor," or "I don't want to be sick," since Spirit cannot "not be," it only recognizes the frequency of "poor" or "sick." It responds to your frequency, not the words you say, so gives you more of "poor" and "sick."

To create a better future, affirm positive thoughts that you can actually believe. Instead of proclaiming, "I am abundant," and feeling you don't have enough money, declare, "I am open to receiving all the money I need!" You can believe that and can be open, so affirm it. And look at all the ways you are abundant in other areas: in the friends you have, the possessions you have. Look at how abundant nature is, how abundant other people are, and recognize it wherever you see it even if it's not yours. It's all the same energy, and when you start loving all expressions of energy, you are no longer blocking any expression of it.

When you surrender to your real Self, you also surrender the free will it has given to the physical personality, subordinating it to the will of Source. In victim consciousness, you have no free will; others impose their will on you. In victor consciousness you claim your free will, exercise it to manifest your desires, but create from a place of separation from Spirit. In vehicle consciousness, you bring through you the desires of Spirit, which have become your desires. They will now appear in your world as physical manifestations of the qualities of Spirit. This process is dynamic; you keep bringing into your life new qualities, or a higher level of the same ones. That's the spiritual evolution of the character you are playing in this lifetime. Your Spirit already is all of those qualities; the character you are is uncovering and visibly manifesting them as circumstances arise.

There Is Never Anything to Forgive

For me, forgiveness is a quality that I am continually faced with, and every time it reveals new depths. I reached forgiving the murder of my son through accepting "I don't know why," which allowed me to dissolve judgments and see the Mind of God working through that situation, so there was nothing to forgive. Next came gratitude that someone had agreed to play the role of the villain for me to reach a higher understanding, plus whatever other gifts there were for my son–for him or for others–of which I had no knowledge. Another level to reach is sincerely praying and wishing the perpetrator the very best rather than trying to forget him–which never works.

Still another level to be explored is that forgiveness is never needed for any person or any circumstance, but can be done for the very first false belief you created eons ago: that you are separate from God, your Source. When you forgive yourself for that original core false belief from which stem all problems, then through the principle of Oneness everyone else is also forgiven, even before there being anything to forgive in the physical world. You never have to forgive any wrongdoing – you forgive the false belief that caused the misdeed through self-forgiveness. And that is profound.

There is nothing in life that's unbearable–if you think that, it's a perception. The proof is you have gone through it and are still here. Discovering the infinite mind of Spirit with the finite mind is impossible. Surrendering to a higher intelligence that loves you unconditionally–so much so it has incarnated in you–seems to be the only logical way to live a peaceful and fulfilled life in spite of its challenges. So for you now, what is the area where you feel stuck or the most resistant? If there are many, just feel into one for now, and we'll do an exercise to help you surrender into that larger life.

Process for Surrendering

Ken Stone, a dear friend and colleague, gave me the process I share here. It's powerful, and I trust it will lead you to a consciousness that is exactly what you need at this time, as it has done for me. From victor consciousness you will be stepping into vehicle consciousness, being just a conduit for the will of the divine. It's always a step into the unknown.

If you are ready for that step, what you will be doing today is first bringing to mind a situation, or an area in your life, that is causing you the greatest distress, and then looking at everything you're afraid of, every scenario, until you get to the worst possible one, after which your feeling will be: "There is nothing worse than this, nothing else I'm afraid of!" Then you focus on that worst outcome and fully accept it as reality. Before, the scenarios were just *possibilities* of what might happen; now, you embrace that worst one as *reality*. The more you let go of control around that situation, the more you will experience the divinity that is You.

PROCESS

Take a few deep breaths, pausing a second or two between the inhale and exhale. Be completely present with your breath, having no intention, just knowing that with each inhale you're receiving the divinity that permeates everything. As you pause at the top of the breath, in that still place take a listening attitude and feel the response of divinity in your body. It can be anywhere and may be any sensation: tingling, twitching, pressure, or waves washing through you. Become aware of any sensation that comes in that moment of stillness, of no thought. Become aware that as you exhale, you are giving to all the life around you what you have just received from divinity–not only its qualities but also, in a very real, physical sense, you are giving to all nature the carbon dioxide it needs so as to transform it back into the oxygen necessary for you to live. You are an indispensable part of the whole ecosystem of your planet. You and all nature are continually receiving and giving the breath of divinity.

And now, bring to mind that most difficult, or most painful situation where you think you have to keep control or bad things will happen. Become aware of the tension around that topic and decide you are ready to surrender it to the wisdom of your Spirit. You, of your own self, simply don't know what else to do. You've tried everything, and nothing seems to work. Surrender to a higher power–a higher intelligence is the only avenue still open. How do you surrender? Let all the scenarios come up, one after the other, everything you fear. Imagine them fully, with all the details. Look at each situation as reality, not just a vague future possibility:

"Now it has happened. My partner has left me."
"I am bedridden for the rest of my life."
"My child has transitioned."
"I'm on the streets now."

Whatever it is for you, feel it as if it had happened: you're in it, and you are being in that situation. Just feel it fully now. And from this place of energetically *being* in the situation, ask yourself again, "What am I still afraid of?" And you might uncover another fear, another scenario hidden underneath.

Redo this process as many times as you find another, even worse scenario. For example: "I'm afraid of having to move to another location, then of not being able to pay my bills, of not having money to buy food or to pay rent; then I'll be out on the streets, a beggar, hungry. Then I won't get medical care, and just lie under a bridge and die without anyone knowing . . ."; consider all the things that come up. There seems to be no end to those scenarios your mind conjures up. You discover new aspects of yourself: you are that homeless person, that poor or abandoned person, that diseased or handicapped person; you are that aspect you don't like, the violent or manipulative one. And it's now coming into your awareness for recognition, to be loved and accepted as an integral part of you. Since it's in your consciousness, it's a part of you. From each new place of fear, keep asking, "From this place, what am I still afraid of?"

When you get to the core fear, the one at the bottom of them all, you can honestly say, "In this place there is nothing more I'm afraid of. Nothing!" And then completely embrace that aspect of you, feel it, be with it. Experience it as your reality. In the acceptance of that worst outcome, let your fear, anger, sadness, frustration, or anguish be expressed in whatever way; through tears, sobs, screams, or punching pillows. Let those emotions and that fear be fully felt, fully expressed, and fully accepted as part of you.

Through shining the light of your consciousness on all those scenarios, you have placed them on an equal footing with the positive aspects of your life. You have brought unity within yourself, no more fighting anything.

If there is still a feeling in you of "I can't accept that," or "I don't want this to happen," remember you always have choice. This is an exercise in surrender you have chosen to do, and you can stop it and choose differently at

THE POWER OF SURRENDER: RELEASING ALL RESISTANCE

any time. You are always in charge. But if you want to step to the next level, and your biggest fear has energetically become your reality, then there is no reason for holding on to control; no reason to fight anything any more; surrender now feels like relief. That's how you will know you have integrated those aspects that were in separation. They are now on your team, working for you and with you. You know God's perspective is perfect, so you let Spirit be your driving force.

To help you really anchor this exercise, imagine you're the driver of the bus of your life. It's going downhill and you're at the steering wheel. At the bottom, the road curves to the left, and straight ahead there is a precipice. You have to keep control of the bus if you don't want it to end at the bottom of the 1,000-foot ravine. If you let go of the wheel, that's exactly what will happen; the bus will keep speeding downhill and over the edge. Now you embrace that worst scenario, accept as real the crash down the cliff. See yourself crushed inside the wreckage; there can be nothing worse.

So what you will do now is give over the control of your bus to Spirit. You will let go of the wheel, get up from the driver's seat, and walk to the back of the bus, all the while asking the divine to take control. You don't have to wrestle with the wheel, and you don't have to make your life go some particular way. You give all control over your life, or one aspect of your life, to the divinity you know you have inside. You surrender, let go of the wheel, and sit in the back, asking the divine to steer the bus. You completely relax, and perhaps remember the song "Jesus, Take the Wheel." And you sit on a back seat, having fully committed to releasing control and to completely accepting whatever happens, including the crash. Feel totally at peace and relaxed because you have relinquished control and turned it over to the part of you that can be absolutely trusted to act for your highest good. Any outcome will be totally welcome.

Surrender Is Ongoing in Every Area of Life

Surrendering and letting go of control is an ongoing practice; you don't just do it once, and it's done forever. You can surrender on every issue that comes up for you, in any area of your life. There is no guaranteed physical outcome for you when you have surrendered other than a feeling of relief, of "all is well," and of peacefulness around your issue. Sometimes there can be an immediate, positive, even to the point of appearing miraculous, outcome. I experienced that when after a month of trying to sort out the issues around leaving Africa, I sat in the middle of the living room and relinquished to the divine all striving and struggling to make things happen. I was totally at peace with no expectations; and that afternoon, every issue was resolved without my lifting a finger.

But usually, the shift in your feelings is the only immediate result, and whatever else comes can only be seen in retrospect. But that shift has raised your vibration enough for you to start seeing things from a higher perspective. That will again lift your frequency. Bit by bit, you will have raised yourself out of the ditch you were in.

That feeling of relief you experience is a profound coming into union with your soul; you know that whatever happens is perfect. Completely open yourself up to feeling it, allowing it to permeate your whole body and mind. The more you stay in that feeling, the more you move from a place of separation to incorporating your soul, from a place of duality into wholeness, a place that feels like home, and like all you've always been and had but just didn't know it. Now that you also know it, feel serene and at peace.

THE POWER OF SURRENDER: RELEASING ALL RESISTANCE

Separation Is an Illusion

Although we look separate from each other, we are all part of the same underlying energy, connected to each other and to everything else. We are indispensable parts of the system called Earth; without you, Earth would be incomplete. Our purpose in this world is far grander than our small individual lives have led us to believe. There is a bigger idea unfolding here that we are not able to perceive with our limited human awareness. My life in Africa had a deep impact on me. I loved being there from the very first moment I stepped off the ship that took me to Lagos; and that is certainly not an experience shared by many. I may have left Africa, a melting pot of so many different races and cultures, but what Africa represents has never left me.

Think of a grand, exotic banquet being prepared by the cook for the enjoyment of his family and friends. It's a colorful, tasty, exotic meal made up of many different ingredients, which the cook gets together in a very large kitchen and starts preparing according to his secret recipe.

All the ingredients have been lined up: one item has to be marinated, so it gets put into a bowl to soak; the nuts have to be cracked, the coconut shredded, the potatoes, onions, tomatoes, and other vegetables are to be peeled, cut up, sliced, mashed, or pounded to a paste. The spices, chutney, coconut, and curry are all put into separate bowls to be used when their time comes; a bottle of palm oil is added to the containers standing ready for use.

Now let's expand the metaphor a little—let's imagine every ingredient has self-consciousness, and therefore has its own thoughts about itself and about everyone else. Therefore, it also has an opinion and an attitude about what's happening. Possibly, it also has an opinion about its own importance, not necessarily shared by the other ingredients. To the cook, every ingredient is just as essential as all the others to make his meal into an extraordinary banquet.

But the ingredients have no idea of what the cook has in mind—none! They only know who and what they are. They think they know what is happening—they see they are peeled, sliced, and mixed—but they don't know the recipe or what the final meal is going to be. Only the cook knows that. They are just separate ingredients with self-consciousness; they are curious, inquisitive, and expectant. They watch and notice things, and have their own ideas about what they want. They anticipate that the result of getting them all together will be something really tasty and outstanding. They are happy to contribute, bringing their special flavor to this grand banquet.

The cook knows it will be some time before the shredded coconut will be needed. So into the refrigerator it goes, complaining, "I was the first to be prepared, and now I'm being shut away in this cold, dark place. I don't like it! Things are going on in the kitchen, but I'm unappreciated, unwanted. I'm sad, miserable, and alone when everyone else is having fun!"

Now the tomatoes are getting upset because when the onions went into the pot, they expected to follow: "We've been waiting forever, we should go next, it's unfair!" The potatoes are hurting since their skins have been taken off; they never expected such pain. The nuts getting their shells cracked believe their lives are falling apart; those that are getting roasted in the oven are moaning about the heat. The grains being soaked feel like they're drowning, and the coconut cream is screaming, "I'm being whipped! It hurts! What did I do wrong?"

They are all experiencing a lot of confusion, pain, and mixed emotions. And guess what? In addition to self-consciousness and attitudes, they also have free will, and now some of them are backing out: "No! I don't want to participate. This is too hard; I never signed up for this!" So the cook has to go and get other tomatoes or potatoes and prepare those, so the whole meal gets delayed, and everyone has to wait a little longer. Do you see what the cook is faced with, and where all this is going?

The meal will get cooked, regardless of the attitudes, the lamenting, and the resistance of the ingredients. The cook knows what's needed for the best result; he's the only one who knows the recipe. If they all got their way, the nuts would not want to be cracked, the cream to be whipped,

THE POWER OF SURRENDER: RELEASING ALL RESISTANCE

the onions drowned in oil, and what you would end up with would be a bunch of separate ingredients, nice enough in themselves, but never the banquet planned by the cook. However, when they all yield to their greater destiny and potential, regardless of the trials they go through, they cease being separate and become something so much more than they could have imagined. They all become one, a culinary masterpiece that brings so much value, joy, and nourishment to all.

Our lives are exactly like that. We are all ingredients in a grand meal, a great masterpiece we cannot even imagine while we're separate pieces of it. When there is no resistance to what's happening, the banquet will come about much sooner, while the journey will be easy and allowing rather than painful and difficult. When it feels like our protective shells are being cracked open, that we are disregarded, unloved, or punished–from our limited perspective–it looks like some crazy chaos is going on. But when we're willing to surrender to a higher idea held by the Divine Cook who's making this meal, then we understand that we're being invited to become part of a great unfolding that nourishes the whole Universe. As we surrender, we discover we're not separate people living just for ourselves, but have a place in a much larger context.

Review of chapter 6:
- ❖ You can live a good life by co-creating it with Source; but to live beyond what you can imagine, you have to surrender your wants.
- ❖ There are four main stages of consciousness, from victim to unity, and they are not linear; we fluctuate between them.
- ❖ Surrender is not giving up; it's focusing on what Source wishes to accomplish in the world through you. It's becoming an instrument for divinity to express.

CHAPTER 7

THE POWER OF A GREAT LIFE: ACTIVATING YOUR POTENTIAL

Will was a little boy with a dream. But Will wasn't growing very much, wasn't outstanding in school or in sports, and since the time his parents took him to a circus, all he dreamed of was becoming a clown. That was not acceptable to his family, who had a high social standing and prominent lives. They also had great expectations for their son, so were becoming rather ashamed of his lack of ambition and not living up to their standards. Will retired into his shell and tried to make himself invisible, but as soon as he was old enough, he just went and joined a circus! His parents told everyone he had gone abroad, and no longer even wanted to speak about him. Will felt unloved, unwanted, and rejected, but loved being a clown. Before every performance, he went to chat with the children who were there early, and played funny tricks to make them laugh.

One day, he saw a sad little girl and asked what was the matter. She said she wished her sister could be there to see him, but she was very sick in hospital and couldn't come. So Will said that after the performance, he would go with her to the hospital and show her sister all his tricks. And that's what they did. Will did all his best tricks and made all the children in the ward happy and forgetful, for a few moments, of their pain and distress.

When the circus moved on, in every new town they visited he always set aside an evening to visit a children's hospital and do a mini-performance just for them. That filled Will's life. He no longer felt sad about being rejected by his family. When he retired from circus life, he just kept on displaying his talent in every place that needed some joy and happiness, so that others could forget all their troubles for a time. And that made him really happy. No one ever knew his name, what he really looked like without his costume, or who he was. But the joy Will had given to countless children lived on through them, their families, and their children, throughout all future generations.

You started out in life with the fullness of Spirit and all its qualities already in you as potential to choose and activate those that appeal to you most. As you grew, both in your body and understanding, you changed and adjusted your ideas and desires, always striving for more. On a deep level, you know your soul is infinite and you will never get to the end of what it has to offer.

You were born with the ingrained determination to never give up. Does a baby who is crawling give up trying to stand up? After all, it has been trying for months with no success. The baby, who has no sense of separation either from Spirit or its parent until approximately the age of two, knows it can do anything and has its parent right there, demonstrating it can be done. This early determination to get the desired result is lost along the way, through the adult wanting to protect the child from harm, and by saying you can't do this or that. The dreams of a child, who thinks he's an astronaut, or riding a unicorn, are cute and encouraged; however, when they get older, they're told to sit and do their homework instead of escaping into unreal fantasies. Later they're told to study something that will give them a high-paying job and that they will never make a living as an artist. Or, whoever heard of wanting to live in a jungle with monkeys? That's ridiculous!

Living a great life means living your dream, doing what you most want to do, and sometimes it starts very early in life. I heard of a girl who loved falcons and from the age of about five hardly talked of anything else. She had heard the story of a falcon in the desert and was fascinated. As she grew, she read all she could lay her hands on about falcons, wanted to live with them, train them, look after them. Her parents discouraged her with visions of how there's no money in that, not even the semblance of a job anywhere in Europe. They felt that going to an Arab country, where falcons are revered as almost–or even better than—humans, was out of the question. Yet this girl never abandoned her dream and ended up with her own hospital, caring for ill or ailing falcons somewhere in a desert, and if I'm not mistaken, in Saudi Arabia. She is known far and wide by the population, and her services are in great demand.

Other times, one's real life purpose is revealed late in life, after having had a "normal," uneventful, or even successful life–but still feeling unfulfilled. That was the story of Neale Donald Walsch when struggling in his fifties, without a job or a home, in bad health, and with no family support. He felt there must be something more to life than both the successes he had had and the challenges he was now experiencing. Discouraged, and with nowhere to turn, he started his private conversations with God. What he heard from God led him out of his desperate struggle into a whole new life filled with ease, simplicity, and joy. Sharing the wisdom he received with the world made him the spiritual leader he is now. So it's never too late, not for any of us, whatever our age or circumstances.

Regardless of What You've Been Through, Start Again

As you go through life and encounter challenges, one thing you never lose is the potential for having the perfection of your Spirit being expressed in your experience. You lose material things, abilities, or capacities through wars, natural disasters, abuse, and accidents; however, you can, if you're willing, re-create a new life. Some people do, some don't. Your mindset and your awareness of the connection you have with Spirit determine the choices you make. So even if someone's done all the great work of the previous chapters, for many people there is still a final obstacle to really living their full potential, their best vision, and their greatest life. This obstacle is their core beliefs about themselves. Those look like: I'm too old, or too young; I've been through too much; I'm tired; I don't have the capacity or the education; I don't have enough time, money, energy, support; I've tried, and it didn't work so why would it work now?; or whatever your excuse is. But now you also know that none of that can actually stop you if you're willing to use your challenges as opportunities to grow, to become more, and to be the best version of you that you can be.

We have countless examples of survivors of wars, concentration camps, or abuses putting their hardships behind them, having a vision of a better life, and manifesting it. We also have many places in the world where people live to a very advanced age, still in good health and contributing to society. I have heard of a tribe in a remote part of Russia where there's no medical care to speak of, and life is hard by our standards, and very simple; many of them are over one-hundred-and-twenty years old and still contributing in their community. Look at the Hunza tribe in a high, remote valley in Pakistan, only accessible over one dangerous and difficult pass. Their terraced gardens are only accessible by foot. There are no roads, and they never had wheeled carts. Yet they seem to have a mindset of mind over matter, and do not view themselves as old when they become seventy or eighty. "Age has nothing to do with the calendar"[1] is a quote from one of their more enlightened rulers.

Spirit's Ways of Operating Are Not Understood by a Human Mind

In your everyday life, when facing struggle and challenges, you might still be stumbling over some limiting beliefs transmitted to you by your parents, teachers, or what you thought you saw in life. Examine the beliefs you are still holding, whether it's about getting a disease because it runs in your family or about not getting a job because you are not qualified for it. I disproved the latter for myself: I was hired for my first job in Africa when I had absolutely no qualifications or experience in forestry and logging. Two years later I was fired because I had discovered many irregularities with the accounting and discrepancies between what was logged and what was sold, and reported it to my boss. This may sound illogical to you, but that's how things work in that part of the world! I had to get fired so that I would have the experience of working in Africa, without which I could not be sent out there again as an expatriate, so that I could meet my future husband and have all my other experiences. Carefully look at what your beliefs are, especially in the areas of your challenges, to see whether they are really true for you. Modern science has been disproving many ideas held by previous generations. But I believe it's also your intuition, your gut feeling, that something is not right or not true, that counts more than even the scientific proof.

Any time you have a health issue, experience the death of a loved one, a divorce, or your home gets reduced to cinders, it does destabilize you for a while. Friends and family can help you initially, but deep down you know it's up to you to rise out of sadness, incomprehension, or despair and restart your life. So long as you have a life, even a handicapped or bedridden one, there is still something that your soul wants you to accomplish–or you wouldn't be alive. But do you know what the desires of your soul are?

Your soul is you, so its desires for you are your desires. But notice that mostly, what you want is the thing you don't actually have right now! Your deepest desires represent the qualities your soul wants to express but cannot until you consciously recognize them in yourself and let them flow out into your world. You are being given right now the experiences you need in order to grow to the level where those desires can be visibly manifested. Abandon the attachment you have to having what you want in exactly the way and at the time you want it. Accept everything that shows up, whether you like it or not, with the mindset that it's an opportunity for you to respond to a situation in a more loving, more compassionate way than ever before, and that will raise your vibration and gradually make you a person whose expansion will be supported by the things you receive. They will not become the next things you are afraid to lose.

You May Not Get What You Want, But Will Always Get What You Need

> What Spirit wants is union with you. It already knows it is you, now you have to realize it too.

Spirit wants to see you only experience realities that are the most direct ways for you to learn, grow, and become the person you need to be; to enter into the next phase of your life where everything you desire, and so much more you're not even aware of, is stored for you and will become yours, as soon as you're spiritually ready. So the most beneficial focus right now is not "Am I getting what I want?" but rather, "Am I using each moment, each experience, as an opportunity to become what Spirit wants me to become?" Life wants you to become more honest in your relationships, both with yourself and others, and more honorable, considerate, and transparent in your daily interactions. Life is helping you expand and perfect the highest qualities and characteristics of your being, to become the most loving, authentic and compassionate expression of Spirit.

You can abandon the belief that if only you get what you want you will be happy and everything will work out. Put aside the belief that you understand how, and as what, your desire needs to manifest. Instead, hold fast to the belief that you are always meant to receive everything you want, but maybe not at this time or in this way. When you visualize your desires and feel the joy of having them in your body, your mind and body are working together just to remind you of what is meant to be as soon as you are congruent with it. Then, you let go of the picture in your mind and just stay with that feeling of joy, happiness, and gratitude permeating your whole being.

What Spirit wants is union with you. It already knows it is you; now you have to realize it, too. Open the door from your side. That comes through releasing any attachment to outcome and allowing Spirit to give you what you want, and much more, but on your soul's terms and conditions.

If you sink into despair and depression, or you're feeling stuck and not knowing where to turn, it's because you don't truly know you are that Spirit, which doesn't perceive your challenges. Spirit cannot be limited by your idea that having lost a limb or your sight or hearing, or not knowing what to do, can in any way prevent it from shining its full light through you into this world. None of those things have the power to prevent you from living your greatest life, but will assist you in getting stronger, more flexible, compassionate, and understanding of Truth; they are a part of living your greatest life.

Truth Is Not Found in the Material World

Now I would like to show you a way to bring yourself back to knowing the Truth.

Look at an area where you think you're stuck, where it's too late or just impossible. It's hopeless to even try. Well, it may be. Perhaps you've lost a leg in an accident. Maybe you've just gone blind. Maybe you've lost all your savings, or your partner has left you. Maybe it's some diagnosis. It seems there's nothing you can do about these facts. But is there really nothing you can do at all?

Notice where the issue or the challenge you are facing is situated. It is always squarely in the human physical realm. Whether it's to do with your work, your family, your finances, or your body, it's all to do with your material life. But you know you are more than your physical body. You are also a Spirit that's just having a human experience. So far, you have been thinking only as a human being; the first shift is to start seeing things more from the perspective of Spirit.

So bring yourself back to knowing the Truth, activating it within you. Know that Spirit or God is omnipotent, omniscient, and omnipresent, infinite and eternal. That means there is nothing that is not an expression of that Spirit, so you are it. Since it is all love, joy, harmony, strength, freedom, health, wealth, genius, beauty, happiness, and an abundance of every good thing, you are also all those things. Spirit loves you unconditionally, and because it has incarnated in you, you have access to all its qualities, which are dormant until you activate them. You can be happy, free, prosperous, and wealthy regardless of your physical state. As best you can, bring to mind every truth you know about God, and know it is the truth about you. Get to the feeling of it being true, so maybe you can say:

"I absolutely know there is only one Presence, one Power, one Mind that is governing everything and expressing its wholeness, completeness, and perfection as, and through, everyone and everything and therefore, also through me. There cannot be anyone or anything that is lacking or diseased

or limited in any way since God is all there is. I AM the full activity of God that is all joy, all harmony, all perfection, all peace expressing everywhere, flowing through every cell of every being, every creature and all of creation. No false beliefs or thoughts of unworthiness, fear, doubt, or anxiety can stay within me when I have consciously activated the Light that is my Source and see it flowing through me, and as me, in every circumstance of my life. Nothing except my own thoughts can stand in the way of the all-pervading perfection of God, and I am now activating the Truth, that every being is a luminous expression of divinity who has the wisdom and knowledge to completely restore and renew itself on every level, known and unknown. I know I am One with the all-powerful Spirit that I AM, now and forever."

This is not an exercise. It is a prayer. Your prayers have gone beyond asking for just material stuff, and you have realized God is in you and is you, so there is no point in asking God to give you anything – you already have it all, but don't yet recollect it.

When you have remembered that, felt it, activated it, stay in that deeply resonant space. Perhaps you even have a sense of relief as your problems have receded a little. You feel a bit more peaceful, and your anxiety has diminished; you're starting to feel that all will be well. Don't let in any doubts or fears; as soon as they surface, bring yourself back again to knowing the Truth, closer to the frequency of Spirit. This does not mean you never take any action. You take action, but now it's inspired action through the connection you have just made with the divine, not action from a place of resistance and desperation, which can only lead to an even more difficult situation.

Rooted in Source, Your Vibration is High

Activating your connection with Spirit raises your frequency to a higher level than when you were feeling unfairly treated, unloved, or the victim of circumstances. You now have access to more positive thoughts, and are able to ask different, more empowering questions, such as: "What's the opportunity in this, to be or do something more, something better?" or "How is this serving me?" You can do this because you know that as Spirit, you have designed this scenario for yourself as the most direct path for your evolution to the next level. You don't remember it now, but you know it's true. So you don't resist, don't fight, but instead keep asking:

- ❖ "What is God's vision for my life now?"
- ❖ "What do I need to change in myself?"
- ❖ "What more can I become, what divine qualities can I demonstrate?"

Just contemplating such questions, not even trying to answer them, will lead you to some insights, to some action you can take to either correct the situation, or give a new direction to your life.

By shifting your perceptions just a little and surrendering your wants to embrace the desires of Spirit, you raise your frequency out of the range of your issue and access solutions that were not apparent to you before. At first, they are perhaps only partial solutions. But from there, if you keep not resisting and asking empowering questions, and then acting on the insights and guidance you receive, you will lift yourself higher and higher until you get to the place where that problem can no longer exist.

What do your challenges look like when compared to those of Helen Keller, who became deaf and blind at nineteen months? This caused her to become mute, as well, and made her interactions with the outside world extremely limited and difficult. In spite of her handicap, she obtained a university degree and wrote a number of articles and books, including an autobiography, *The Story of My Life.*

What do your challenges look like when compared to the story I shared in an earlier chapter of Nick Vujicic, born without arms or legs? Think of all the people who, through accidents, war, or being blown up by minefields, have become paralyzed or lost limbs, but are still functioning and being of service to others in whatever ways they can, in spite of their handicaps.

Look at what Stephen Hawking has overcome, the disease ALS, amyotrophic lateral sclerosis, which gradually paralyzed him. At the age of twenty-one, he was given two years to live. But he pursued his studies in mathematics, astronomy, and cosmology, obtaining a doctorate. With his physical state getting worse, he still did research leading to his Big Bang theory and black hole studies, while also a professor at the University of Cambridge in physics and astronomy. He also married and had three children. Progressively paralyzed and incapable of feeding himself or getting out of bed alone, his elocution got so distorted he had to have a special computer built, with a voice synthesizer to read what he wrote. This allowed him to keep lecturing at Cambridge. Now, over seventy years old and with only the muscles of his lips and eyebrows functioning, he is a brilliant physicist, cosmologist, mathematician, and also a writer. His determination to keep living a fulfilled and productive life in spite of all his handicaps and inability to speak is awe-inspiring.

A New Cycle of Time Started in 2012

We have developed all manner of strategies and ways of dealing with our challenges, both individually and globally, which have worked well for us so far but may no longer work in the future because they are unsustainable in the new energy that is being broadcast to the earth since we entered a new cycle of time in 2012. This subject is vast, and not within the scope of this book; however, we must become aware that the times we are living in are unprecedented and very pivotal ones. The earth is changing, moving into a new dimension, and we must change with it. We are at the end of what Gregg Braden calls a "world age" and starting the next "world age," the sixth in the history of humanity. These cycles are normal, and we have had four of them, only remembered through legends and myths. The fifth is the 5,125 years ending in 2012, and each time a cycle closes, humanity has been almost totally destroyed.

This time humanity is still here, and in 2012 we started a new cycle of 5,125 years on a higher spiral of evolution. What we have learned from our parents and what humanity knows from ages past may not be serving us now; solutions may not work as they used to. This time, humanity has survived the shift of the ages. Yet in order to thrive, new, different, untried, and sometimes counter-intuitive solutions to world problems–as well as for your own problems–must be found. People are very resilient and we have a built-in mechanism for survival, but it's not "survival of the strongest" as was taught by Darwin in his *The Origin of Species*.

Science has now proved this to be a false assumption, but our economic systems and corporations still run on that understanding; that's why they are unsustainable. Darwin's conclusions that nature shows us patterns of survival of the strongest animals and plants being in competition with each other are false. On the contrary, nature shows us cooperation between species, and even between plants and insects. So we have to totally rethink our old ways of doing things. We must find renewable sources of energy instead of using oil and find ways to stop pollution. It's best to cease wasting the resources we have and curb the continual drive for more profit at the expense of the well-being of people, nature, and Gaia herself.

> Spirit has provided us with free will and focus, which is like the dial of a radio, so we can choose the frequencies we want to listen to and live in.

As an example, when we see overhead power lines being continually broken by severe winter conditions, instead of just repairing them, we might consider burying them underground where they would not be affected by hurricanes and ice. The initial high cost of sustainable solutions would be worth the effort, because the next "world age" into which we have just entered is on a higher, spiritual spiral of evolution. We must leave the old world and start a new one on a solid, sustainable basis.

An Individual Can Influence Global Issues

Those are global considerations, and, as individuals, we have little or no control over them. Where we do have control is over our own back yard and over the items we buy. We could stop waste and recycle everything we can. Use paper bags rather than plastic ones and recycle the paper. Buy organic, to encourage farmers to stop polluting the soil with chemicals. If you are willing, there are countless ways to improve your habits. If people stop buying a certain product, it will soon stop being produced, and "people" starts with you. That is really important. Yet what about the mental, emotional, or physical side of you? If your dreams of a better life, success, an ideal partner, or health are not manifesting, let's look at why.

It may be it is your continual thought of "it hasn't yet manifested, it's not here" that is holding it away from you. This is why your desire is not manifesting; you're looking at the appearance and continually re-creating that. But remember, you also recognize the Spirit that is you has everything available right now, and all you have to do is tune in to that Spirit. Just as you know you are surrounded by radio waves all the time, but if you want to hear the music, you have to have a radio and tune the dial to the frequency that plays your favorite music. Similarly, in the material world you are surrounded by frequencies carrying divine qualities such as love, harmony, joy, generosity, and abundance–and also frequencies generated by human beings, carrying the false and limiting beliefs of lack, limitation, disease, poverty, anger, and fear, among many others. You must tune in to the frequencies that you want.

Spirit provided us with free will and focus, which is like the dial of a radio, so we can choose the frequencies we want to listen to and live in. We must choose to become aware of the frequencies of Spirit; activate them in ourselves through our thoughts, feelings, and actions; and then radiate those qualities out into the world and to the people around us, both by intention and action. The world acts as a mirror, reflecting back the qualities we radiate out. But if we choose to focus on anger, resentment, or disease—the world still acts as a mirror, reflecting back the negative thoughts we give out. By matching your vibration with that of your soul, you have access to all the qualities your dream represents. Eventually they will solidify into a manifestation of your desire, unless you push them away each time you think "Why are they not here yet?"

> There is no good or bad energy. Energy just IS.

Your own imagination can only come up with a dream that enhances the best experiences you have had so far, but the divine ideas for this life are beyond your imagination. Aligning with your soul and asking for its plans to be fulfilled through you makes miracles happen.

Your Soul Doesn't Know Your Age and Doesn't Care

Remember your soul, that divine power, doesn't know your age, gender, or circumstances; and it doesn't care or know anything about the challenges you've created for yourself. All the soul knows is that it's now incarnated in the world and wants to express all it is into that world. That's the agenda of your soul, and it doesn't know anything about timing. It cannot see anything that is a limitation, a problem, or anything less than itself because the soul is all Light, and Light cannot see darkness. When conditions are right, its potential can unfold, and you are creating those conditions by your thoughts, beliefs, and actions. Your soul is timeless, infinite, immortal, and eternal, and is only concerned with its own perfection, which is infinite and indivisible until it's expressed. It can then be broken down into various qualities such as harmony, joy, peace, patience, security, and abundance that, when unified, become Love, or "perfection." All qualities spring from love, a state of being rather than a feeling or an emotion. Love is like an ocean upon which arise waves of feelings–some gentle and peaceful, some angry or destructive–but the waves never cease to be a part of the ocean. Within the context of time and space, they arise and pass, transform, transmute, and sink back into the depth of the ocean that is love.

While everything in nature expresses Source in a more limited way, you and I have been given a higher awareness of our spiritual identity and the free will to choose which qualities of Spirit we wish to express at any given time. As spiritual beings, we are timeless and infinite; however, as human beings we are locked into a finite world of time and space that we call duality.

Your free will lets you choose which facets of duality you wish to act out: the anger or forgiveness, confidence or lack of it, selfishness or regard for others. The world then allows you to see the results of your choices. Note that none of these are wrong in and of themselves. They are just energy expressed, and there is no good or bad energy. Energy just IS. The way we use energy is the thing that matters. You use it according to the consciousness you have in any given moment, and what the world reflects back allows you to see whether you have used the energy in accordance with universal will, or in opposition to it–in other words, using energy in a good or not so good way.

Since there is a time lag between your actions and the reflected image, it's not always easy to see the correlation between the two;

however, if you don't like some aspects of your life, you know the area in which to make adjustments in your perceptions, thoughts, and finally actions.

We Are the Instruments through which Source Plays Its Music

When your human consciousness is aligned with the divine consciousness within you, you become a Light. As soon as Light appears, darkness is no more. Darkness is not a thing in itself; it's an absence of Light. When it says in the Scriptures, "In the beginning was the Word, and the Word was with God, and the Word was God. All things were made by Him; and without Him was not any thing made that was made," (John 1:1) that is the perfect, eternal, invisible, and spiritual creation. God being perfection only creates perfection. So He did not create darkness; if He had, darkness would be the nature of God, eternal, unchanging. Where God is, Light is, and there is no place where God is not. That's the meaning of Omnipresence. Darkness can only manifest where Light has been obscured by false beliefs. When a cloud obscures the sun, darkness results. But the cloud does not stop the sun from shining, and the sun only sees its own Light, not the darkness below caused by the cloud. The Light doesn't do anything to the darkness. It doesn't clear it out, release it, or chase it away. The sun dissolves the cloud, and darkness simply has no more existence where there are no more clouds. That's the meaning of the phrase ". . . the darkness and the light are both alike to thee." (Psalms 139:12)

You are that Light, even if it's temporarily obscured by your human qualities. So regardless of what you've been through, or what you are still going through now, regardless of your age, your sexual orientation, or any other material fact about you, this power within you has the ability to express its potential and its greatness through you. But you must allow it. Become aware of that, use your free will to cooperate with the grandeur of your soul, and be willing to bring out the love it is.

You are the instrument through which your soul has chosen to play its music. Do you care how old your guitar is? All you care about is how it sounds when you play it, and how it's rendering the music you feel inside. Sometimes it's soft and melodious, sometimes strong and tumultuous, but always beautiful, always a perfect expression of what you're feeling. All your soul cares about is how you transmit all it is into the world. Without that instrument–your body, the soul could not express itself. So take good care of your body, and make it the most perfect you can, so the music of your soul can be poured through you. Although, when the time arrives that the instrument can no longer adequately serve the musician, another instrument must take its place. So do not be overly attached to the instrument, because You, the musician, will be playing the music of your soul eternally, through a variety of instruments. Identify with your soul, that expression of divinity, more than with your body.

Consider what our soul is in relationship to that infinite Source. We are just sparks of light flickering on and off as we go through our various incarnations, never separate from that infinite expanse of All That Is. We, and everything else in the universe, are an expression in visibility of that infinite, invisible energy that we call the divine. It created a pure expression of itself as our soul; our physicality is just a concept that our soul laid on the canvas of space and time. The soul, that spark of Light, will always be expressing itself once here, once there, and eternally, or it will be resting in its Source between incarnations. However, when you identify with the body, you think you only live for seventy to eighty or so years. That's only a belief. And a belief only holds true as long as you believe in it.

The Body Obeys the Commands of the Mind

Our soul is unlimited in every way, while our bodies and minds are limited by the space/time construct we are born into and through our beliefs. In the Middle Ages, the average life span was forty, and now it's double that or more. What changed? We think it's because of better medical care and better life conditions. That, certainly, has helped shift our beliefs in the area of longevity. But there are documented cases and whole tribes of people living longer lives than our present average without any medical care to speak of and in really hard conditions. They have been like that for centuries–and are largely untouched by Western civilizations. Their beliefs shape their reality; our beliefs shape ours, even if external circumstances may have some influence.

There is a documented case when a doctor told someone that she had a terminal illness, so to put her affairs in order as she had a month to live. She did that and actually died at the end of the month. Later, it was discovered that her medical file had been confused with another one, and so actually, she did not have the terminal illness of the other patient. Why did she die?

I know of another case when a person died in a scenario he agreed to participate in, where he was told his veins had been opened and he would bleed to death within four minutes. He actually died at the end of the four minutes, although his veins were intact.

So our beliefs shape our material reality; they do not change Truth or spiritual reality that is one and unchanging. Take the example of reincarnation: many people believe in it, many people don't. A number of organized religions have even outlawed holding that belief. But when scientific proof is brought in to uphold a certain belief, little by little more and more people believe in it, more and more facts are observed to uphold that belief, and if it reflects Truth, that belief will become established. More and more proof supports the idea that the soul reincarnates into different bodies, and that it can bring remembrance, knowledge, and abilities of previous or, rather, parallel incarnations. When you add the fact that your soul has all the qualities of Source within it in potential, and it's up to you to activate that potential, then anything becomes possible.

Bringing Knowledge from Past Lives Is Possible

A few years ago, I heard the story of a three-year-old boy, I believe in the Golan Heights, who knew he had been murdered in a previous lifetime and kept repeating it. In the end, his parents went to the local authorities and asked for it to be verified. The boy told them the name of the murderer, the name of the neighboring village where it had happened, and showed them the place where his body had been buried. He also said that the ax with which he had been killed was in the tomb. When the police started digging, they found the skeleton of a man and also the ax. They arrested the murderer, who broke down and confessed to his crime.

Look at Mozart, a child prodigy, who composed his first symphony at the age of six. He was considered extremely talented, and since his sister was also an accomplished musician, it was thought they inherited those abilities. That may have been a contributing factor, but you cannot inherit more than your parents have; his abilities, at the age of four, far surpassed those of his parents. Now we can consider the fact he was remembering another incarnation and bringing in the talents he had already developed that were stored within his soul. We have many documentaries, even YouTube videos, showing children who come with abilities way beyond what we consider "normal," and with skills that are considered "learned" skills, not inborn abilities.

We Need Not Be Limited by Beliefs and Genetics

And in a different register, people we consider "old" are starting new careers, or starting to do things they had never done before.

They are taking university courses in physics, astronomy, medicine, mathematics, or whatever, at an age when the expectation is they can no longer learn, their memory is not what it used to be, or their neural pathways are set in certain ways and cannot change.

Science is now proving that our cells are designed to regenerate themselves almost indefinitely. Bruce Lipton, a world-renowned author and medical doctor, proved, with his research on cells and DNA, that we can live far longer lives than we actually do. His book *The Biology of Belief* is a groundbreaking testimonial that it is not our cells or our body that determine the life of the body, but a spiritual broadcast from beyond the body. He is the founder of the science called "epigenetics," that is, "above genetics"–meaning we are not subject to the laws established by our genetic component, but have the power to void what our genetics may indicate by our thoughts, beliefs, and, ultimately, actions. It's our Spirit that governs all the functions of the body, right down to life itself.

What Is a Great Life

So now, let's define a great life. It doesn't mean great achievements or what the world calls great: making millions of dollars, becoming the president of your country, or having your photo on the cover of *Time* magazine. Movie stars, considered so great, often lead disastrous lives. Even bedridden and handicapped, your life, if you will allow it, will reflect the spiritual qualities and activities of your consciousness; and greatness resides only in the way you are a reflection of the qualities of Spirit.

The world may never hear of you or give you any recognition, but you have lived a great life as a mother or a father if you've brought up your children to be heart-centered, responsible, kind, and happy citizens, and a credit to their family and community. Challenges don't prevent you from living your greatest life; often, they are the cause for living it; as in the case of a woman whose daughter was in a coma and she just sat by her for years, caring for her, just loving her. People began to visit her house, simply to be in the energy of love that was so thick it was palpable. She had activated such a sacred consciousness of love and service that just being in her presence in this situation was transcendent and healing.

Living a great life might mean discovering talents you never suspected you had and developing them so you could be of service to others, or might mean rediscovering ones you had abandoned because of a busy life caring for your family. A dear aunt of mine, her children grown up and scattered all over the world and her husband having passed on, took up cross-stitching and beautifully reupholstered some antique chairs. She could have easily made her living doing that, but her eyesight became too weak to sew, and she took up painting. Her works still decorate her son's home, as well as those of other members of her family. Then she was diagnosed with glaucoma and went blind. That did not stop her. At eighty years old, she turned to sculpting, taking courses, and living her life fully until the end. She was an example of a happy and fulfilled life to her children and grandchildren.

And even look at my own story, which took me through the WWII years in Poland, years in business in Africa, many losses and challenges resulting in a deep spiritual search that led me, at the age of seventy-five and against much resistance, to being of service through energy healing–something I knew absolutely nothing about.

Recognize Who You Really Are and Radiate That

The power to live your greatest life goes much deeper than just winning awards and becoming publicly recognized as a success. It may include that, of course, but it's not very often the case. Basically, it has to do with being true to yourself and true to your spiritual nature, even if you never accomplish anything noteworthy in terms of what the world considers great. Most "great" lives are lived by ordinary people in ordinary circumstances who face their problems and difficulties with courage and integrity, and who are an example of patience, understanding, and harmony to their children. They are wise and supportive in their communities and bring joy and inspiration to everyone they meet.

Regardless of material accomplishments, if you live your life in a spiritual consciousness, you are activating and unleashing a very transcendent power into the world. That is a tremendous blessing to everyone and every particle of life anywhere that is in your awareness. Because consciousness is One, and if your consciousness reflects Truth and your true nature, no matter what your circumstances, then that will be extending out through the quantum field to all life that is ready to be uplifted by it. So living a great life is not what most people think; it's not fame, it's not fortune, and it's not material success. It's living a life of service to others and being rooted in the Truth of your Being. As written in *Conversations with God*, "Your life is not about you. It has nothing to do with you. It has to do with everyone whose lives you touch, and the way in which you touch them."[2] And in the words of Martin Luther King: "Anybody can live a great life, because everybody can serve."[3]

You can feel that life is calling you, charging you to go and make a difference wherever you are planted at the moment. Everyone is being called, but few are answering the call because it means doing the work to become strong enough to carry that higher purpose, that vision. But I know that since you are still reading, you are willing to fully show up and shine your light exactly where you are, regardless of your situation, or what circumstances look like. You have grown into the consciousness of Yes I can! Yes I'm able! Yes I will! Yes I AM!

When you do that, you will be living your full potential. A rose hidden in a hedge doesn't stop blooming because there is no one to see it, and doesn't stop releasing its fragrance because no one will appreciate it, but rather it opens just for the joy of being that beautiful rose. And the same is true for you. Whatever you are facing, or whatever the world thinks, the power and the blessing you have activated in your own sphere of activity, however big or small, will continue to live eternally in the hearts of those close to you, and will expand through them all the way around the world. Living your greatest life is doing what you love doing most, not for the rewards it may bring, but just for the joy of it. Whether it's painting on canvas that will bring beauty into a home for centuries, or painting on a sidewalk that will get washed away with the next rain. Whether it's sculpting a marble statue, or an intricate design on a watermelon that will get eaten the next day. Whatever brings you joy will spread the consciousness of joy to the world around you. The words "It's not what you do, but how you do it that really matters" have the ring of perennial truth; and we would do well to take them to heart.

A Final Challenge

My challenge to you right now is to bring to mind the highest vision for your life, the one that you have defined and refined many times while reading this. And commit, really commit, to this: that every day, and for the next forty days, you will do something towards your vision. One thing, every day, holding the intention: *"This is going to further my vision!"* Whether it's writing, making sales calls, exercising, having a conversation that needs to be had, meditating–the activity will change, but it must be something towards incorporating your highest vision into your life. It's important to state your intention and say it out loud, if possible, so that all your cells hear it and take it into their consciousness. Your sincere intention for engaging any activity, even seemingly unrelated, will start anchoring that intention into everything you are doing. Then watch as that vision unfolds, and at the end of those forty days you will be at a level you never thought possible. Then rest in wonder and awe–and gratitude to *Yourself*–for achieving your highest vision.

That is living a great life.

Review of chapter 7:
- ❖ Spirit loves you unconditionally and has given you all its qualities, but it's up to you to activate them.
- ❖ Spirit knows nothing of your age or circumstances, your problems or limitations: Light cannot see darkness.
- ❖ No matter what you're facing, if you are willing to own and activate your divinity, align with Source, and stay true to who you really are, you will be a blessing to all life. That power of blessing will continue to live on, eternally.

ABOUT THE AUTHOR

Jania was not always a transformational energy healer; that's a relatively recent chapter in her life. Born in Poland before WWII, Jania only knew war and strife during her childhood and early teens. During her adult life in West Africa, she was in the midst of civil wars in the 1960s. But her life tragically changed after her husband died in a plane crash and after her only child was murdered. There was no more human logic to lean on, an impossible forgiveness to be found, and she had to search deeper than ever in order to survive.

Challenges have always shaped Jania. She escaped Poland with her mother and siblings to settle in England, where she finished her education. Longing for adventure, Jania found a job in Nigeria with an import/export company, where she met her Swiss husband. For about thirty years, they lived in West Africa, where their only son was born. It was partly an enchanted life, visiting game parks, going on safaris, and living close to nature, even if always in capital cities. And it was partly a difficult time, living in the midst of civil wars or ethnic disturbances in one country after another, following the independences in the 1960s. That idyllic life came to an end when her husband died in a plane crash. Jania left Togo, where her husband was then stationed, to start a new life in Switzerland, a country she didn't even know.

Between the grief of losing her husband, raising a thirteen-year-old boy alone, and trying not to sink into despair, Jania had to discover inner resources, which didn't seem to exist outside. She began a path of spirituality, which would become her guiding force. Years later, her son was murdered–as fate would have it–also in Africa, and died in a coma just as her husband had.

Jania had to be the one to remove her son's ventilator. At that point, something cracked open. There was no more hope, no one to live for. She knew something had radically changed.

Jania searched for the real reasons why things happen. She studied, read, prayed, and meditated. At one point, at the age of seventy-five, she was "gifted" with the clear knowledge that she was a healer– something she knew absolutely nothing about. She committed to it instantly, with just one caveat. She said aloud to God, "You have to bring me everything I need, as I don't even know where to begin." As a result, the condition of her foot that looked like gangrene, and which no doctor could remedy completely, disappeared overnight.

In the next few years Jania's life changed from just spiritual learning to becoming an energy healer. The modalities she needed have always been miraculously brought to her; she never had to search for anything. Her private healing practice organically developed into a business–something she never really wanted. It led to writing this book, then to a radio show, and it seems like her life is one continuous stream of starting to do things she knows absolutely nothing about, each one leading to the next.

And who knows what her next assignment is going to be? Jania's commitment is to heal, awaken, and transform all beings to create a world where people respect, value, and appreciate each other and all creation. A world that works for the highest good of all.

For more information, please visit Jania at www.JaniaAebi.com.

NOTES

Chapter 1
1. N. J. Dawood. *The Koran* (Penguin Classics, 2015).
2. "Your Wishes Fulfilled, with Wayne Dyer." *Jennifer McLean's Healing With The Masters Season 12,"* Podcast audio, November 7, 2013.
3. Derek Rydall said that this is the definition of the Sanskrit word for "human."

Chapter 2
1. I heard this on a call with Derek Rydall, who has worked with Michael Beckwith extensively.
2. William Ernest Henley, "Invictus," *A Book of Verses* (Nabu Press, 2010).
3. Ibid.
4. Albert Einstein, brainyquote.com.
5. Derek Rydall's definition of *man* from ancient Sanskrit.

Chapter 3
1. Bruce Lipton, *The Biology of Belief: Unleashing the Power of Consciousness, Matter & Miracles* (Hay House, 2016).

Chapter 4
1. Albert Einstein, brainyquote.com.
2. Jonathan Bender said this to me in a private conversation about a talk that I was creating.
3. Derek Rydall's "The Law of Emergence" program.

4. Neale Donald Walsch, *Conversations with God* (TarcherPerigee, 2005).

Chapter 5
1. The 7 Sacred Gifts came from a program and live calls by Derek Rydall.
2. Mahatma Gandhi, brainyquotes.com.

Chapter 6
1. I have heard Derek Rydall say this many times.

Chapter 7
1. This saying is attributed to the Hunza tribe, the longest-living people who reside in the Hunza Valley on the border of Pakistan and India.
2. Neale Donald Walsch, *Conversations with God* (TarcherPerigee, 2005).
3. This is an excerpt from his sermon "The Drum Major Instinct." Martin Luther King, Jr., *A Knock at Midnight: Inspiration from the Great Sermons of Reverend Martin Luther King, Jr.* (Warner Books, 2000).

RESOURCES

Braden, Gregg. *The Divine Matrix: Bridging Time, Space, Miracles, and Belief.* Hay House, 2008.

Brown, Michael. *The Presence Process: A Journey into Present Moment Awareness.* Namaste Publishing, 2010.

Capra, Fritjof. *The Tao of Physics: An Exploration of the Parallels between Modern Physics and Eastern Mysticism.* Shambhala, 2010.

Carroll, Lee. *Kryon—The End Times: New Information for Personal Peace.* Kryon Writings, 1993.

Easwaran, Eknath. *The Bagavad Gita.* Nilgiri Press, 2007.

Germain, Saint. *The I Am Discourses.* Saint Germain Press, 1989.

Gordon, Richard. *Quantum-Touch: The Power to Heal.* North Atlantic Books, 1999.

Hay, Louise L. *You Can Heal Your Life.* Hay House, 1999.

Herriott, Alain and Jody. *Quantum-Touch Core Transformation: A New Way to Heal and Alter Reality.* North Atlantic Books, 2009.

Hicks, Esther and Jerry. *Ask and It Is Given: Learning to Manifest Your Desires.* Hay House, 2004.

Katie, Byron. *Who Would You Be Without Your Story?: Dialogues with Byron Katie.* Hay House, 2008.

Lipton, Bruce. *The Biology of Belief: Unleashing the Power of Consciousness, Matter & Miracles.* Hay House, 2016.

Melchizedek, Drunvalo. *The Ancient Secret of the Flower of Life.* Light Technology Publishing, 1998.

Papastavro, Tellis S. *The Gnosis and the Law.* New Age Study of Humanity's Purpose, Inc., 1972.

Rydall, Derek. *Emergence: Seven Steps for Radical Life Changes.* Atria Books/Beyond Words, 2015.

Schucman, Helen. *A Course in Miracles–Original Edition.* Course in Miracles Society, 2006.

Spalding, Baird T. *Life and Teaching of the Masters of the Far East.* DeVorse & Company, 1986.

Sterling, Fred. *Kirael: Lemurian Legacy for The Great Shift.* Lightways Publishing, 2006.

Tolle, Eckhart. *The Power of Now: A Guide to Spiritual Enlightenment.* Namaste Publishing, 2004.

Twyman, James F. *The Moses Code: The Most Powerful Manifestation Tool in the History of the World.* Carlsbad: Hay House, 2010.

Vitale, Joe. *Zero Limits: The Secret Hawaiian System for Wealth, Health, Peace, and More.* Wiley, 2008.

Walsch, Neale Donald. *The Complete Conversations with God.* TarcherPerigee, 2005.

Wattles, Wallace D. *The Wisdom of Wallace D. Wattles: The Science of Getting Rich.* SoHo Books, 2012.

Weissman, Darren R. *The Power of Infinite Love & Gratitude: An Evolutionary Journey to Awakening Your Spirit.* Hay House, 2007.

Whitworth, Eugene. *Nine Faces of Christ.* DeVorse & Company, 2012.

Yogananda, Paramahansa. *Autobiography of a Yogi.* Crystal Clarity Publishers, 2005.

www.ingramcontent.com/pod-product-compliance
Lightning Source LLC
Chambersburg PA
CBHW071608080526
44588CB00010B/1067